The Bahá'í Faith
in Words and Images

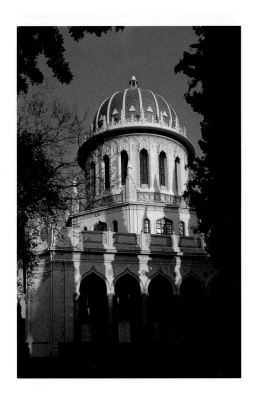

The Bahá'í Faith
in Words and Images

JOHN DANESH and SEENA FAZEL

with PHOTOGRAPHS by PAUL SLAUGHTER

ONEWORLD

The Bahá'í Faith

(founded in 1844)

If this is of God it will endure; if not, it can do no harm.

QUEEN VICTORIA (1869)

If he [Bahá'u'lláh] is God, I am three Gods.

NAPOLEON III (1870)

Very profound. I know of none other so profound.

LEO TOLSTOY (1910)

The Bahá'í Faith is a solace to mankind.

MAHATMA GANDHI (1944)

Bahá'ísm is an independent religion on a par with Islam, Christianity, and the other recognised world religions.

ARNOLD TOYNBEE, HISTORIAN (1959)

[Bahá'ís] are a political faction; they are harmful. They will not be accepted.

AYATOLLAH KHOMEINI (1979)

One of the newest of the great universalist religions, Bahá'í warns us ... to properly regard the relationship between humankind and nature.

AL GORE (1992)

Contents

INTRODUCTION   8

CORE BELIEFS   14

CENTRAL FIGURES   30

SACRED TEXTS   56

GOD AND PROPHETS   72

BODY, MIND AND SPIRIT   84

COMMUNITY LIFE AND
ORGANIZATION   96

CONTEMPORARY
CHALLENGES   128

THE BAHÁ'Í FAITH IN
THE TWENTY-FIRST CENTURY 146

ART AND
ARCHITECTURE   114

FURTHER READING   156
INDEX   157
ACKNOWLEDGEMENTS   160

introduction

THE BAHÁ'Í FAITH, founded by an Iranian nobleman called Bahá'u'lláh (1817–92), is an emerging world religion. Its main teachings are that all people share a common spiritual origin and dignity, and that religious history should be viewed as a continuous process guided and inspired by one ultimate source, which some religions have called God. Although the Bahá'í Faith shares certain features with Judaism, Christianity and Islam, its beliefs and practices distinguish it as an independent faith. At the beginning of the twenty-first century Bahá'ís number some six million worldwide, and they are found in virtually every country and territory. They represent a broad cross-section of humanity, with followers representing most racial, ethnic and social backgrounds. The phrase 'unity in diversity' is

main picture The Shrine of the Báb on Mount Carmel, Haifa, Israel.

left Detail of the shrine, displaying a Bahá'í symbol of spirituality.

sometimes used to describe the sheer variety of Bahá'í membership, and many illustrations in this book reflect this characteristic. Bahá'ís live ordinary lives, working, studying and raising families in mainstream society. They cannot be identified by any particular marking,

above and opposite Members of the Bahá'í community represent virtually every racial, ethnic, and social background. After Christianity, it is the world's most widely spread religion.

clothing, or habit, and their faith has nothing in common with charismatic or secretive movements described as 'cults'. Those unfamiliar with the Bahá'í Faith are struck by its attitude of critical optimism. Bahá'í teachings tend to combine idealistic principle with pragmatic policy. Perhaps this can be illustrated with two examples: the Bahá'í Faith teaches that human nature is intrinsically good but supports legal systems based on justice. The faith also promotes disarmament and world peace, but argues for practical measures, such as collective security agreements between nations, to help make these ideals real. But perhaps the faith's most unusual feature is its lack of major division. For more than a hundred and fifty years there has been an unbroken chain of succession in the faith's leadership. It is partly this internal unity that enables Bahá'ís to envisage the possibility of global harmony. This book attempts to provide a concise

overview of the Bahá'í Faith's teachings and history, its contemporary situation and its likely prospects in the near future. Although readers might better understand the early history of the faith with greater information about nineteenth-century Iran and Islam, we have reduced such discussion to focus on issues most relevant today. Also, to avoid overburdening the reader, most English versions of Persian and Arabic words appear with minimal accents and other markings. The selected reading list contains references for the material that we cite, and also provides interested readers with sources that give more detailed accounts of topics only briefly reviewed here.

Distribution of Bahá'ís

- Over 100,000
- Between 10,000 and 100,000
- Between 1,000 and 10,000
- Under 1,000

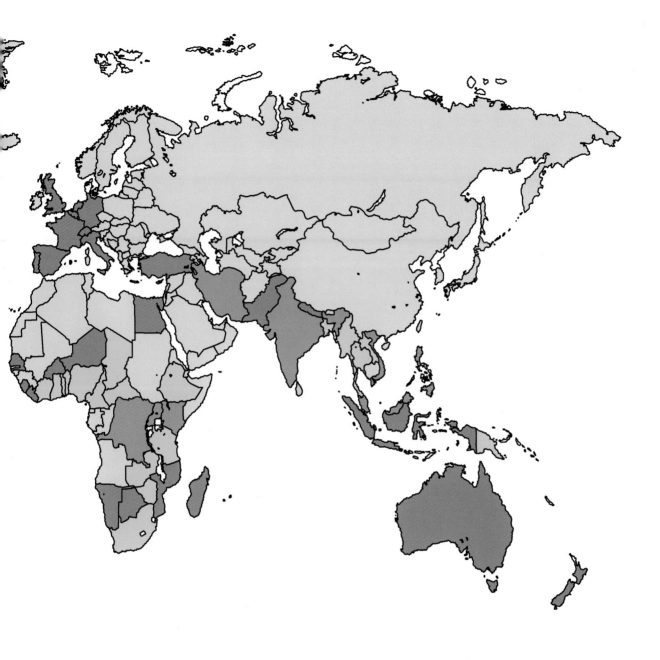

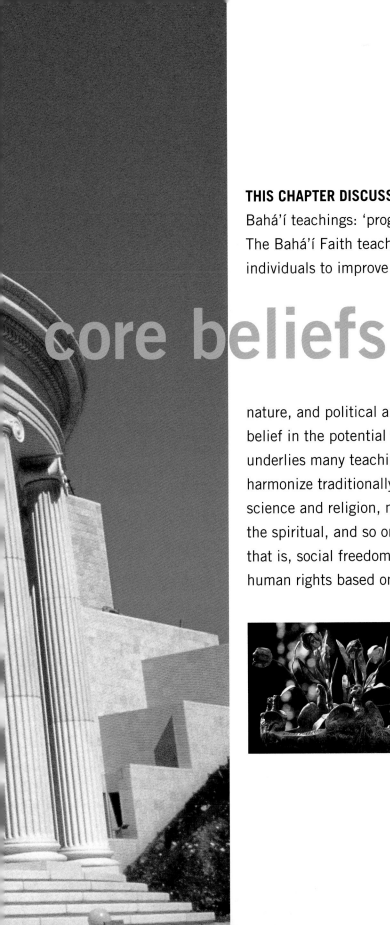

core beliefs

THIS CHAPTER DISCUSSES THREE IDEAS at the core of Bahá'í teachings: 'progress', 'harmony' and 'freedom'. The Bahá'í Faith teaches that the purpose of life is for individuals to improve their spiritual nature, and that the development of the human soul continues in the afterlife. In addition to personal spiritual development, Bahá'í views on religious history, nature, and political and social trends all reflect this belief in the potential for progress. The idea of 'harmony' underlies many teachings, encouraging Bahá'ís to harmonize traditionally difficult relationships: between science and religion, men and women, the material and the spiritual, and so on. Bahá'ís also advocate 'freedom' – that is, social freedoms such as increased liberty and human rights based on justice.

main picture Centre for the Study of the Texts, Haifa, Israel.

left Detail of the garden ornaments, Shrine of the Báb.

opposite Passage from the writings of Bahá'u'lláh, founder of the Bahá'í Faith.

Progress

The idea of progress connects Bahá'í beliefs on subjects as diverse as the purpose of life, religious history, the human soul, and even global order. In particular, Bahá'ís credit many achievements in human history to the civilizing influence of religion.

Upon the reality of man, [God] hath focused the radiance of all of His names and attributes, and made it a mirror of His Own Self. These energies ... lie latent within man, even as the flame is hidden within the candle and the rays of light are potentially present in the lamp.

(BAHÁ'U'LLÁH)

Individual progress

The Bahá'í Faith teaches that each individual possesses both a physical body and a unique and eternal essence called the human soul or spirit. The nature of this essence is mysterious. The soul is both a spiritual and an intellectual reality that is not satisfied with material comforts alone: it seeks something more, something beyond itself.

Bahá'í texts explain that divine qualities are latent within the human soul, just as the colour, fragrance and blossom of a flower are latent within the seed. Cultivation of the soul entails a lifetime of effort, involving the love and knowledge of God, acts of generosity and the development of spiritual qualities such as honesty, humility and self-sacrifice. Participation in family life, education and service are also ways of developing the soul. These efforts should be seen as shaping rather than trying to change human nature, for Bahá'ís believe that people are essentially good.

Bahá'ís believe that the development of the soul continues after death, although it is not possible to understand the afterlife, just as a baby in the womb of its mother cannot understand the outside world. Bahá'í writings do, however, explain that there are no physical places of 'heaven' or 'hell'. There is no existence previous to life here on earth, nor is the soul reborn several times in different bodies, but the attributes acquired during a human lifetime will assist the soul's progress forever.

A SUMMARY OF VIRTUE

Be generous in prosperity, and thankful in adversity.

Be worthy of the trust of thy neighbour, and look upon him with a bright
  and friendly face.

Be a treasure to the poor,

  an admonisher to the rich,

  an answerer to the cry of the needy,

  a preserver of the sanctity of thy pledge.

Be fair in thy judgment, and guarded in thy speech.

Be unjust to no man, and show all meekness to all men.

Be as a lamp unto them that walk in darkness,

  a joy to the sorrowful,

  a sea for the thirsty,

  a haven for the distressed,

  an upholder and defender of the victim of oppression.

Let integrity and uprightness distinguish all thine acts.

Be a home for the stranger,

  a balm to the suffering,

  a tower of strength for the fugitive.

Be eyes to the blind, and a guiding light unto the feet of the erring.

Be an ornament to the countenance of truth,

  a crown to the brow of fidelity,

  a pillar of the temple of righteousness,

  a breath of life to the body of mankind,

  an ensign to the hosts of justice,

  a luminary above the horizon of virtue,

  a dew to the soil of the human heart,

  an ark on the ocean of knowledge,

  a sun in the heaven of bounty,

  a gem on the diadem of wisdom,

  a shining light in the firmament of thy generation,

  a fruit upon the tree of humility.

BAHÁ'U'LLÁH

Progress of religion

Bahá'ís believe that a single universal being ('God' or Ultimate Reality) has inspired all world religions. God intervenes from time to time in human history, but only indirectly through enlightened intermediaries or prophets. Bahá'ís regard these individuals, such as Moses, Jesus, Buddha, Muhammad and Bahá'u'lláh, as teachers of one universal faith, and only incidentally as founders of different religions (see p. 76 for further details). On spiritual matters these prophets have spoken with one voice and have shared a common purpose:

Is not the object of every Revelation to effect a transformation in the whole character of mankind, a transformation that shall manifest itself both outwardly and inwardly, that shall affect both its inner life and external conditions? (BAHÁ'U'LLÁH)

[The Bahá'í Faith's] teachings revolve around the fundamental principle that religious truth is not absolute but relative, that Divine Revelation is progressive, not final ... It proclaims all established religions to be divine in origin, identical in their aims, complementary in their functions, continuous in their purpose, indispensable in their value to mankind. (SHOGHI EFFENDI)

Certain aspects of religions have, however, varied depending on their audiences. As societies mature, prophets are able to give them more advanced social teachings, promoting further social progress. As individuals develop their spiritual powers, they come to understand more deeply the spiritual insights of prophets.

Know of a certainty that in every Dispensation the light of divine Revelation hath been vouchsafed to men in direct proportion to their spiritual capacity. Consider the sun. How feeble its rays the moment it appeareth above the horizon. How gradually its warmth and potency increase as it approacheth its zenith, enabling meanwhile all created things to adapt themselves to the growing intensity of its light ... Were it all of a sudden to manifest the energies latent within it, it would no doubt cause injuries to all created things ... In like manner, if the Sun of Truth were suddenly to reveal, at the earlier stages of its manifestation, the full measure of the potencies which the providence of the Almighty hath bestowed upon it, the earth of human understanding would waste away and be consumed; for men's hearts would neither sustain the intensity of its revelation, nor be able to mirror forth the radiance of its light. (BAHÁ'U'LLÁH)

Bahá'ís explain instances in history when religion has contributed to human misery as distortions of faith provoked by corruption and fanaticism.

Social progress

While many regard religion as purely a personal matter, Bahá'ís believe that it has guided not only the individual's spiritual growth but also social progress. Bahá'í writings broadly describe a pattern of gradual improvement in social history and envisage a future society organized as some decentralized, global confederation of states. This is needed because some issues, such as conflict between nations, and certain economic, environmental and health problems, can best be resolved with international cooperation. Bahá'ís believe that people should see beyond narrow nationalism (although they regard a 'sane and legitimate' patriotism as healthy). They should, instead, value the larger good of humanity.

Bahá'í writings state that this next leap in the world's social evolution is not far off, describing symbolically how humanity has passed through 'infancy' and 'adolescence' and is now approaching collective 'maturity', a time characterized by the 'emergence of a world community, the consciousness of world citizenship and the founding of a world civilization and culture' *(Shoghi Effendi)*. Bahá'ís, therefore, see a definite direction in social history and correlate the goal of social progress with that of the individual. Hence, Bahá'ís are encouraged to make efforts in their own personal lives that will enable them to 'carry forward an ever-advancing civilization' *(Bahá'u'lláh)*.

Nature's progress

Another aspect of the Bahá'í idea of progress involves nature. Bahá'í writings indicate that science offers the most appropriate way of answering questions such as 'How was the universe created?' or 'Did humans evolve from other creatures?' Bahá'í texts do, however, make some comments that generally support the idea of gradual progress in nature.

For example, they state that the earth's physical characteristics have evolved over time, as has humankind:

Man, in the beginning of his existence and in the womb of the earth, like the embryo in the womb of the mother, gradually grew and developed, and passed from one form to another ... until he appeared with this beauty and perfection, this force and power. It is certain that in the beginning he had not this loveliness and grace and elegance, and that he only by degrees attained this shape, this form, this beauty and this grace. ('ABDU'L-BAHÁ)

Harmony

Harmony The Bahá'í belief in the ability of individuals and societies to improve leads naturally to another core idea. Bahá'ís see as their ultimate goal the creation of a just society based on a 'new world order': 'Soon will the present-day order be rolled up, and the new one spread out in its stead' (Bahá'u'lláh, 1868). This 'golden age' will appear only after the world's most serious conflicts and injustices have been resolved, not only those between nations or religions but also those between women and men, black people and white, rich and poor. Sometimes Bahá'í writings comment in detail on how harmony can be achieved in troubled relationships. The general idea is that harmony is possible, but only with an understanding that spiritual truth is one and that all people share a common origin and nobility.

below Bahá'í writings describe racism as 'an outrageous violation of the dignity of human beings'.

Racial harmony

Bahá'í teachings reject racial prejudices as false and unjustified beliefs. The Bahá'í approach to racial harmony involves three steps. The first is to

right Bahá'ís encourage efforts to help overcome the 'grievous and slow-healing wounds of racism'.

understand that differences in skin colour and in other physical characteristics are trivial:

Numerous points of partnership and agreement exist between the two races [i.e. black and white]; whereas the one point of distinction is that of colour. Shall this, the least of all distinctions, be allowed to separate you as races and individuals? In physical bodies, in the law of growth, in sense endowment, intelligence, patriotism, language, citizenship, civilization and religion you are one and the same. ('ABDU'L-BAHÁ)

Even the understanding that racial prejudices are irrational, however, may not be enough to overcome them. The second step, according to Bahá'í writings, involves seeing spiritual virtues in other individuals:

Know ye not why We created you all from the same dust? That no one should exalt himself over the other. Ponder at all times in your hearts how ye were created. Since We have created you all from one same substance it is incumbent on you to be even as one soul, to walk with the same feet, eat with the same mouth and dwell in the same land, that from your innermost being, by your deeds and actions, the signs of oneness and the essence of detachment may be made manifest. (BAHÁ'U'LLÁH)

The final step goes beyond the mere acceptance of different races. It involves a celebration of the variety of forms and colours in the human race: 'Bahá'u'lláh hath said that the various races of humankind lend a composite harmony and beauty of colour to the whole. Let all associate, therefore, in this great human garden even as flowers grow and blend together side by side without discord of agreement between them' *('Abdu'l-Bahá).*

Harmony between women and men

Bahá'ís believe that women and men share the same spiritual status. They are regarded as equal in intelligence and ability. If women have lagged behind men in some respects, this is not due to innate differences:

The difference in capability between man and woman is due entirely to opportunity and education. Heretofore woman has been denied the right and privilege of equal development. If equal opportunity be granted her, there is no doubt she would be the peer of man. ('ABDU'L-BAHÁ)

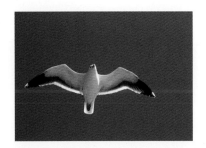

above The wings of a bird are used as a metaphor in Bahá'í writings to illustrate the ideal of balance and equality in relationships between women and men.

Bahá'í teachings, however, go beyond affirmation of gender equality. Men and women should see themselves as 'partners and coequals' *('Abdu'l-Bahá)*. The metaphor of a bird is frequently used in the Bahá'í writings to illustrate this finely balanced relationship: 'The world of humanity has two wings – one is women and the other men. Not until both wings are equally developed can the bird fly' *('Abdu'l-Bahá)*. Men themselves suffer if women are held back: 'As long as women are prevented from attaining their highest possibilities, so long will men be unable to achieve the greatness which might be theirs' *('Abdu'l-Bahá)*. Communities can suffer from these imbalances as well. In fact, Bahá'ís believe that world peace is unlikely until women take leading roles in society.

Bahá'í writings also state that society needs to strike a better balance between qualities traditionally regarded as either 'masculine' or 'feminine'.

The world in the past has been ruled by force, and man has dominated over woman ... But the scales are already shifting; force is losing its weight, and mental alertness, intuition and the spiritual qualities of love and service, in which woman is strong, are gaining ascendancy. Hence the new age will be an age less masculine and more permeated with feminine ideals, or, to speak more exactly, will be an age in which the masculine and feminine elements of civilization will be more properly balanced. ('ABDU'L-BAHÁ)

Harmony of science and religion

The Bahá'í Faith is often described as a 'scientific religion'. This is partly because it lacks a clergy, and its members are encouraged to investigate religious matters through independent and systematic study. It also teaches that science and religion are complementary aspects of human progress: they are seen as different methods of trying to understand the same reality. If 'truth is one', contradictions between inspired religion and valid science can only be apparent ones: 'Whatever the intelligence of man cannot understand, religion ought not to accept. Religion and science walk hand in hand, and any religion contrary to science is not the truth' ('Abdu'l-Bahá).

Bahá'í scripture exalts scientific knowledge: 'Knowledge is as wings to man's life, and a ladder for his ascent. Its acquisition is incumbent upon everyone ... Great indeed is the claim of scientists and craftsmen on the peoples of the world' (Bahá'u'lláh).

The Bahá'í writings offer several approaches to bring science and religion together. The first is to promote a spirit of open-minded investigation: 'In order to find truth we must give up our prejudices, our own small trivial notions; an open receptive mind is essential. If our chalice is full of self, there is not room in it for the water of life' ('Abdu'l-Bahá).

A second approach involves instilling a greater awareness of ethics in scientists. Such understanding might help to avoid disastrous applications of knowledge, thereby saving science from 'the dreary bog of materialism' ('Abdu'l-Bahá). Rational thought, on the other hand, can help prevent the slide of religion into 'the slough of superstition' ('Abdu'l-Bahá).

top Dr Richard St. Barbe Baker, O.B.E., 1889–1982, who became a Bahá'í in London in 1924, was a world-famous environmentalist who founded The Men of the Trees, now called The International Tree Foundation. In 2006, St. Barbe Baker was named by the UK Environment Agency as one of the top 100 green campaigners of all time.

above August Forel, a Swiss psychiatrist, entomologist and social reformer, became a Bahá'í in 1921 after receiving a letter from 'Abdu'l-Bahá outlining Bahá'í views on the existence of God and the spiritual nature of human beings. He is featured here on the Swiss one-thousand-franc note.

When religion, shorn of its superstitions, traditions and unintelligent dogmas, shows its conformity with science, then there will be a great unifying, cleansing force in the world, which will sweep before it all wars, disagreements, discords and struggles, and then will mankind be united in the power of the love of God. ('ABDU'L-BAHÁ)

Another approach involves acknowledging that science and religion address different aspects of reality. For example, on questions related to the origins of the universe or human evolution, people should turn to science, which constantly revises its theories about the natural world in the light of new evidence. Religion may give additional insights into such matters through stories and metaphors, but these should be interpreted symbolically rather than literally: 'This story of Adam and Eve who ate from the tree, and their expulsion from Paradise, must be thought of simply as a symbol. It contains divine mysteries and universal meanings' *('Abdu'l-Bahá)*.

Bahá'ís value scientific endeavour, and its members are well represented in scientific, medical and technical fields, possibly because Bahá'ís see spiritual significance in the achievements of science and technology.

Other aspects of harmony

There are further aspects of the Bahá'í principle of harmony, some of which are discussed later in this book. Bahá'í texts discuss ways in which to promote harmony between the followers of different religions (see p. 78), between family members (see p. 98) and between members of different social and economic groups (see p. 134). Bahá'í teachings also emphasize the need for harmony between people and the natural environment, including a humble appreciation of nature:

Every man of discernment, while walking upon the earth, feeleth indeed abashed, inasmuch as he is fully aware that the thing which is the source of his prosperity, his wealth, his might, his exaltation, his advancement and power is, as ordained by God, the very earth which is trodden beneath the feet of all men. There can be no doubt that whoever is cognizant of this truth is cleansed and sanctified from all pride, arrogance and vainglory. (BAHÁ'U'LLÁH)

Perhaps the most basic harmony of all, however, is an internal one: the balance between the physical desires that impel humans to act selfishly and the nobler aspirations of a spiritual nature. Completeness in life is achieved by the successful resolution of this struggle.

above A Bahá'í kindergarten in Fiji, South Pacific. Schooling and education are described in Bahá'í writings as top priorities, to enable the achievement of human potential.

opposite It is a Bahá'í principle to encourage children to investigate religious truth for themselves, rather than to imitate others blindly.

Freedom
Liberty, but not licence, is at the heart of Bahá'í belief. The more freedom people enjoy, the more opportunities they have to determine their own destiny. Individual freedom is regarded as essential for the fulfilment of human potential, but it should be matched by a strong sense of civic and personal responsibility. Bahá'ís regard the ability to rise above material affairs as the highest form of freedom, thereby allowing concentration on one's inner spiritual life.

Individual search for truth
Bahá'ís believe that the individual's right to unfettered enquiry is the most fundamental of all freedoms: 'There is nothing of greater importance to mankind than the investigation of truth ... Look into all things with a searching eye' *('Abdu'l-Bahá)*. This process should be free from imitation, heredity and blind faith: 'Set aside superstitious beliefs, traditions and blind imitation of ancestral forms of religion and investigate reality' *('Abdu'l-Bahá)*. It is highlighted by the religion's lack of a clergy, for Bahá'ís believe that in the modern world all individuals have the duty and the right to seek truth without interference from others. Such truth-seeking is a lifelong endeavour. The goal for each individual is to explore both the inner world of spiritual potential – to discover one's 'true self' – and the external world of ideas and natural laws. Insight can be gained by the use of various methods, including reason, reflection and intuition (see p. 88).

Basic rights

Bahá'ís believe that all people are born with a number of essential rights related to their personal welfare: the right to adequate food, clothing and shelter; the right to own property; and the right to health care. (Humanitarian centres around the 'houses of worship' are anticipated to provide some of these services; see p. 116.) Great emphasis is placed on the right to education. All boys and girls should, at the very least, be given the opportunity to learn to read and write. When their parents and schools cannot provide this instruction, society should intervene: 'The primary, most urgent requirement is the promotion of education. It is inconceivable that any nation should achieve prosperity and success unless this paramount, this fundamental concern is carried forward' ('Abdu'l-Bahá).

Certain other rights described in the Bahá'í writings affect an individual's social welfare. These include the right to personal safety and, ultimately, to a peaceful world; the right to choose leaders in democratic elections; and the right to seek legal redress and justice, the pursuit of which is regarded as 'the best beloved of all things' (Bahá'u'lláh). Bahá'í texts generally encourage a climate of free speech, freedom of assembly and freedom of the press, but suggest that such freedoms can exist only within the limits of self-regulated moderation. The press is described as 'an amazing and potent phenomenon', but it has a responsibility to reflect events truthfully as 'the mirror of the world' (Bahá'u'lláh).

The individual and society

Bahá'í teachings aim to balance the freedoms of the individual with the collective good. Bahá'í writings support, for example, the idea that people who earn more should pay higher rates of income tax, and that companies should share profits with their employees. Despite the provision of welfare, every individual is encouraged to work. Above all, however, individuals are instructed that serving their communities is a form of worship.

That one indeed is a man who, today, dedicateth himself to the service of the entire human race ... Blessed and happy is he that ariseth to promote the best interests of the peoples and kindreds of the earth. (BAHÁ'U'LLÁH)

Religious freedom

Bahá'í teachings have certain safeguards against religious intolerance. Bahá'í writings contain statements that affirm freedom of conscience, the right to different religious beliefs, or to no religious belief. Bahá'ís are told not to discriminate in any way against those who are not Bahá'ís, and children born into Bahá'í families are free to choose their own spiritual paths.

Just as in the world of politics there is need for free thought, likewise in the world of religion there should be the right of unrestricted individual belief. Consider what a vast difference exists between modern democracy and the old forms of despotism. Under an autocratic government the opinions of men are not free, and development is stifled, whereas in a democracy, because thought and speech are not restricted, the greatest progress is witnessed. It is likewise true in the world of religion. When freedom of conscience, liberty of thought and right of speech prevail – that is to say, when every man according to his own idealization may give expression to his beliefs – development and growth are inevitable.

('ABDU'L-BAHÁ)

Detachment

Bahá'ís regard 'detachment' as the highest form of freedom. Detachment involves freedom from materialism and self-indulgence, although not to the point of extreme self-denial and seclusion from the world. Bahá'ís should live in the world but not become worldly, for the pleasures of the world are for people to enjoy so long as they remain detached: 'On wings of detachment, soar beyond all created things' *(Bahá'u'lláh)*. Bahá'ís do not believe that poverty is a spiritual ideal; rather that spiritual people will contribute to society's prosperity without becoming attached to its material benefits. The expression of detachment is in self-sacrifice, altruism and charitable service to others.

Tell the rich of the midnight sighing of the poor, lest heedlessness lead them into the path of destruction, and deprive them of the Tree of Wealth. To give and to be generous are attributes of Mine; well is it with him that adorneth himself with My virtues. (BAHÁ'U'LLÁH)

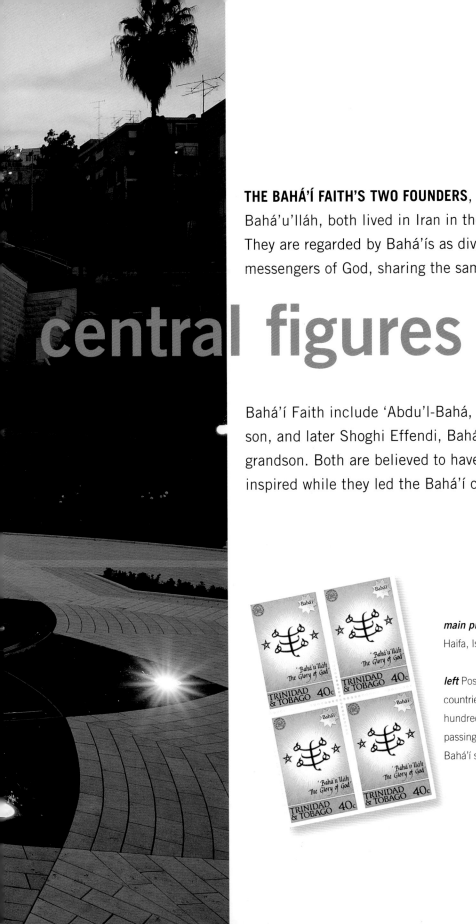

central figures

THE BAHÁ'Í FAITH'S TWO FOUNDERS, the Báb and Bahá'u'lláh, both lived in Iran in the nineteenth century. They are regarded by Bahá'ís as divinely inspired messengers of God, sharing the same status as Zoroaster, Buddha, Jesus and the prophet-founders of other religions. The other central figures of the Bahá'í Faith include 'Abdu'l-Bahá, Bahá'u'lláh's eldest son, and later Shoghi Effendi, Bahá'u'lláh's great-grandson. Both are believed to have been divinely inspired while they led the Bahá'í community.

main picture Shrine of the Báb in Haifa, Israel.

left Postal authorities in several countries commemorated the hundredth anniversary of Bahá'u'lláh's passing in 1992 by issuing stamps with Bahá'í symbols.

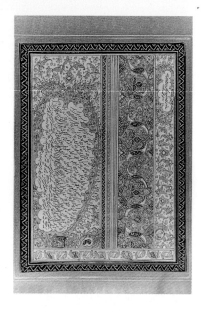

The Báb

Bahá'ís regard the Báb (literally 'the gate') as the prophet-herald of their faith. Within six years of claiming prophethood in 1844, he was shot by a firing squad of the Iranian imperial army. Notwithstanding, he had already attracted tens of thousands of followers and written a number of works that frequently alluded to the imminent appearance of another prophet, 'Him Whom God will make manifest'. The Báb's teachings were radical for their age and his disciples famously heroic. According to Jules Bois, a French literary critic:

All Europe was stirred to pity and indignation ... Among the litterateurs of my generation, in the Paris of 1890, the martyrdom of the Báb was still as fresh as had been the first news of his death [in 1850]. We wrote poems about him. Sarah Bernhardt entreated Catulle Mendes for a play on the theme of this historic tragedy.

The Báb was born Sayyid Ali Muhammad in 1819 in the southern Iranian city of Shiraz. He came from a family of merchants, and had little formal education. His revelations began at a time when widespread expectations of a messiah had gripped Iran. By most accounts, his presence was electrifying. The Báb's first disciple described an encounter thus: 'I felt possessed of such courage and power that were the world, all its peoples and its potentates, to rise against me, I would, alone and undaunted, withstand their onslaught. The universe seemed but a handful of dust in my grasp.' The Báb urged his disciples to be pure and brave:

Purge your hearts of worldly desires, and let angelic virtues be your adorning ... The time is come when naught but the purest motive, supported by deeds of stainless purity, can ascend to the throne of the Most High and be acceptable unto Him.

His teachings challenged Islamic norms, especially his criticism of the clergy's literal interpretations of Islam's holy book, the Koran. He praised scientific advancement and fairness of mind. In symbolic attempts to shatter the prevailing system, he proposed an elaborate system of new religious laws in his principal book, *The Exposition*. He made these proposals, however, subject to the approval of his successor. On numerous occasions he referred to himself as 'the gate' leading to this next messenger. (*The Exposition* contains more than three hundred references to 'Him Whom God shall make manifest'):

I swear by the most holy Essence of God ... that in the Day of the appearance of Him Whom God shall make manifest a thousand perusals of the Bayan [The Exposition] cannot equal the perusal of a single verse to be revealed by Him Whom God shall make manifest.

above Sample of the Báb's handwriting. He wrote about eighty books.

opposite top House of the Báb in Shiraz, a place of pilgrimage for Bahá'ís before it was destroyed in 1979.

opposite bottom Upper room in the house of the Báb where, in May 1844, he proclaimed his prophethood in the presence of his first disciple.

Within a few years the Báb had an estimated one hundred thousand followers, about 2·5% of Iran's population. The clergy were outraged by his religious claims, and his popularity made government ministers fear him as a potential rival. He was arrested and confined to a series of remote prisons. His cause, however, continued to spread: during his stay in Isfahan the city's governor became a follower; during a mock trial in Tabriz designed for his public humiliation he won even more supporters; during the Báb's confinement in the mountain region of Maku, the prison governor became an ardent supporter. His followers soon came under attack, and on a few occasions they were forced to take defensive positions. At three separate sites between 1848 and 1850 hundreds of followers, mostly religious students, artisans and peasants, were surrounded by imperial troops. These sieges followed a similar pattern. For several months the Báb's followers resisted, and even gained notable victories, but eventually they were overcome by superior numbers or by false promises of ceasefires, and nearly all were massacred.

The Báb's own death was as dramatic as his rise. In 1850 the new Shah and the Prime Minister decided that the only way of stopping the Báb and his movement would be to kill him. He was brought to a public square in Tabriz and suspended in front of a firing squad consisting of a regiment of several hundred Armenian soldiers. After a failed execution attempt, a new regiment had to be called, as the first group of soldiers, regarding the failed attempt as something of a miracle, refused to shoot again. The Báb was killed on 9 July 1850.

above Port city of Bushihr where the Báb moved at the age of fifteen to work for his uncle, later setting up his own trading business. He returned to Shiraz after an extended pilgrimage where, aged twenty-two, he married Khadíjih Khanum, who became one of his earliest followers.

right In 1847 the Báb was exiled to Maku, an isolated mountain prison where he wrote several works including his principal book, *The Exposition*.

bottom left The shrine of Shaykh Tabarsi where about three hundred followers of the Báb, mainly students and artisans, were besieged by more than ten thousand imperial troops for seven months in 1848. Almost all were killed after surrendering to the authorities.

bottom right Shrine of the Báb on Mount Carmel, Haifa, where the Báb's remains were brought from their hiding place in Tehran and interred in 1909.

left In 1848 the Báb was exiled to Chihriq, another remote mountain prison, where he spent the last two years of his life.

right Barrack square in Tabriz, where the Báb was executed in July 1850.

below Shrine of the Báb on Mount Carmel, Haifa, as it looks today. Shoghi Effendi commissioned the design and building of the more elaborate superstructure, topped by a golden dome, which was completed in 1953. In the foreground stands the classically designed International Bahá'í Archives building.

O My beloved friends! You are the bearers of the name of God in this Day. You have been chosen as the repositories of His mystery. It behoves each one of you to manifest the attributes of God, and to exemplify by your deeds and words the signs of His righteousness, His power and glory. The very members of your body must bear witness to the loftiness of your purpose, the integrity of your life, the reality of your faith, and the exalted character of your devotion ...

Purge your hearts of worldly desires, and let angelic virtues be your adorning. Strive that by your deeds you may bear witness to the truth of these words of God, and beware lest, by 'turning back', He may 'change you for another people', who 'shall not be your like', and who shall take from you the Kingdom of God. The days when idle worship was deemed sufficient are ended. The time is come when naught but the purest motive, supported by deeds of stainless purity, can ascend to the throne of the Most High and be acceptable unto Him.

(Passages from the Báb's final address to his early followers)

above View of nineteenth-century Tehran, where Bahá'u'lláh spent much of his early life before his exile to Iraq in 1853, aged thirty-five.

Bahá'u'lláh

A Bahá'í is a follower of Bahá'u'lláh (literally, 'the glory of God'), prophet-founder of the faith that now bears his name. Bahá'ís believe that he was the one foretold by the Báb, and regard him also as the fulfilment of prophecies of other religions (see p. 76). Whereas the Báb's career was short and spectacular, Bahá'u'lláh lived from 1817 to 1892, and spent most of his adult life as a prisoner and exile in the Middle and Near East. His extensive writings in Persian and Arabic form the foundation of the religion's scripture.

He was born Mirza Husayn Ali Nuri, the son of a northern nobleman whose ancestors were kings of ancient Persia. Like other members of his class he was educated chiefly in calligraphy, poetry and horsemanship. He refused a ministerial career and, instead, became known locally as 'the father of the poor' for his charitable work. Bahá'u'lláh's privileged existence, however, came to an end in 1844 when he became an enthusiastic supporter of the Báb. He was one of a few noblemen to join the movement (most of the other leading followers of the Báb were religious students and merchants). As a consequence he soon lost his home and possessions. He and his family suffered jeering and beatings by mobs and by the authorities, faced arbitrary arrest, and subsequently suffered hunger, poverty and illness.

During a spate of attacks on the Báb's followers in 1852, Bahá'u'lláh was arrested without charge and thrown into an underground dungeon in Tehran called the 'black pit'. There he had a spiritual experience which, in retrospect, marked the start of his mission, and which resembled the experiences of other religious founders (see p. 76). After his release Bahá'u'lláh was exiled with his family to Baghdad in neighbouring Ottoman Iraq. He soon rallied the dispirited surviving followers of the Báb, and acted as the community's leader. After a few years he retreated to the mountains of Kurdistan for two years, leading a simple life and meeting Islamic mystics. There he wrote the *Seven Valleys*, the best known of his mystical works.

Bahá'u'lláh's religious claims were gradually revealed to the Báb's followers and others. A few devotees realized that he was the messiah foretold by the Báb, but Bahá'u'lláh did not publicly announce this until the eve of his forced departure from Baghdad in 1863. Even then, the declaration was made only to a small group of followers. Some of his writings before that date appear to allude to his future claims, including passages in the *Book of Certitude*, his most important doctrinal work. His first public claim to prophethood occurred in a garden that he named 'Paradise' (Ridván) located outside Baghdad. The anniversary of that date in April is celebrated annually by Bahá'ís (see p. 104). Given the Islamic setting, it was significant that one of Bahá'u'lláh's first pronouncements was to prohibit his followers from waging holy war (*jihad*).

The Shah of Iran pressed the Ottoman government to move Bahá'u'lláh even further from Iran's frontiers to lessen his influence on his Iranian followers. Bahá'u'lláh was therefore banished to Istanbul, capital of the Ottoman Empire, where he stayed for only three months before being further exiled to Edirne, a remote city in European Turkey. There Bahá'u'lláh publicly announced his claim to be the founder of a new religion. He wrote letters to the leading European and Central Asian monarchs in which he encouraged them to be just to their subjects and to investigate the nature of his own claims. At this time Bahá'u'lláh also faced increasing hostility from certain followers of the Báb, including his own half-brother, who sought the leadership of the community. His detractors wrote inflammatory reports to the Ottoman authorities, and this eventually led to another exile – this time to Palestine, in Ottoman Syria, in 1868. Bahá'ís regard the actions of these individuals as reminiscent of the betrayal of Jesus by his disciple Judas Iscariot, and the opposition to Buddha by his cousin Devadatta.

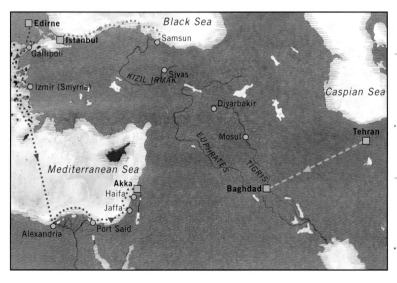

Exile of Bahá'u'lláh from Tehran to Akka

---- First journey from Tehran to Baghdad (12 January–8 April 1853)

.... Second journey from Baghdad to Istanbul (3 May–16 August 1863)

---- Third journey from Istanbul to Edirne (Adrianople) (1–12 December 1863)

.... Fourth journey from Edirne to Akka (12–31 August 1868)

above Sketch of Akka, site of one of Bahá'u'lláh's imprisonments.

below An etching of the cell in Akka prison, where Bahá'u'lláh was incarcerated for two years from 1868.

In 1868 Bahá'u'lláh and the loyal members of his family arrived in the prison city of St Jean d'Acre, now Akka in northern Israel. Bahá'u'lláh was imprisoned in the citadel for two years, and then placed under house arrest for the rest of his life. During this time he wrote extensively, the most notable work being the *Most Holy Book*, his principal book of laws. Towards the end of his life the authorities gradually became less hostile, and Bahá'u'lláh was allowed to move outside the city walls. He received an increasing number of pilgrims, but only a few Westerners ever met him. One of them was E. G. Browne, an orientalist from the University of Cambridge, who had travelled to the Middle East to study this new movement (see panel). Another was Amir Amin Arslan, a Lebanese journalist, who wrote in a French periodical: 'His appearance struck my imagination in such a way that I cannot better represent it than by evoking the image of God the Father, commanding, in His majesty, the elements of nature, in the middle of the clouds.'

When Bahá'u'lláh died in May 1892, 'Abdu'l-Bahá, his eldest son and chosen successor, cabled the Ottoman authorities: 'The sun of Bahá has set.' Bahá'u'lláh's shrine, located next to his final home, is a place of pilgrimage for Bahá'ís.

A PEN-PORTRAIT OF BAHÁ'U'LLÁH

by E. G. Browne

One of the few Westerners to meet Bahá'u'lláh was Professor Edward G. Browne, an orientalist from the University of Cambridge. He has left this description of his meeting with Bahá'u'lláh:

My conductor paused for a moment while I removed my shoes. Then, with a quick movement of the hand, he withdrew, and as I passed replaced the curtain; and I found myself in a large apartment, along the upper end of which ran a low divan, while on the side opposite to the door were placed two or three chairs. Though I dimly suspected whither I was going and whom I was to behold (for no distinct intimation had been given to me), a second or two elapsed ere, with a throb of wonder and awe, I became definitely conscious that the room was not untenanted. In the corner where the divan met the wall sat a wondrous and venerable figure, crowned with a felt head-dress of the kind called táj by dervishes (but of unusual height and make), round the base of which was wound a small white turban. The face of him on whom I gazed I can never forget, though I cannot describe it. Those piercing eyes seemed to read one's very soul; power and authority sat on that ample brow; while the deep lines on the forehead and face implied an age which the jet-black hair and beard flowing down in indistinguishable luxuriance almost to the waist seemed to belie. No need to ask in whose presence I stood, as I bowed myself before one who is the object of a devotion and love which kings might envy and emperors sigh for in vain!

above E. G. Browne, a Cambridge scholar who interviewed Bahá'u'lláh.

A mild dignified voice bade me be seated, and then continued:– "Praise be to God that thou hast attained! ... Thou hast come to see a prisoner and an exile ... We desire but the good of the world and the happiness of the nations; yet they deem us a stirrer up of strife and sedition worthy of bondage and banishment ... That all nations should become one in faith and all men as brothers; that the bonds of affection and unity between the sons of men should be strengthened ... Let not a man glory in this, that he loves his country; let him rather glory in this, that he loves his kind."

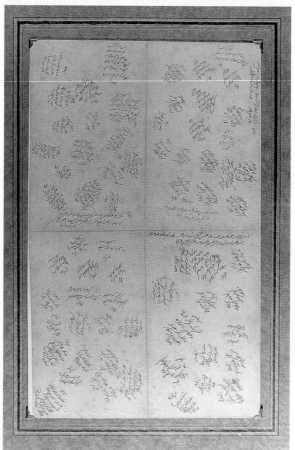

above Mirza Buzurg, father of Bahá'u'lláh and minister to the Shah's court.

above right Some of the verses from the *Hidden Words*, in Bahá'u'lláh's own handwriting. By the time he was forced to leave Baghdad in 1863, Bahá'u'lláh had written two of his major works, the *Book of Certitude* and the *Hidden Words*.

right Baghdad in the nineteenth century. Bahá'u'lláh was exiled here for ten years.

right Akka prison. In 1868 Bahá'u'lláh was sent by the Ottoman authorities to Akka, a penal colony in Palestine at the time, and imprisoned there for two years.

middle The house in Akka where Bahá'u'lláh lived under house arrest after his release from prison in 1871.

below Bahji, a few miles from Akka, where Bahá'u'lláh passed away on 29 May 1892. This is one of the Bahá'í holy places in Israel that UNESCO added to its list of World Heritage sites in 2008.

'Abdu'l-Bahá

'Abdu'l-Bahá (literally, 'the servant of Bahá') was the head of the Bahá'í community from 1892 until his death in 1921. Bahá'u'lláh appointed him in the *Book of the Covenant* as the interpreter of his teachings. Bahá'ís regard 'Abdu'l-Bahá as the perfect example to be followed, but do not view him as a messenger of God. Through his travels 'Abdu'l-Bahá brought the faith to the attention of large numbers of people in Europe and North America, giving public talks on Bahá'í teachings relevant to contemporary issues, including ways to stop religious fanaticism, to promote disarmament and racial harmony, and to protect human rights.

'Abdu'l-Bahá was born in Tehran, reportedly on 23 May 1844, the day that the Báb first claimed prophethood, and named Abbás after his grandfather. From the age of nine, he shared Bahá'u'lláh's years of imprisonment and exile, and later acted as his secretary and deputy. He was finally freed in 1908 at the age of sixty-five when the Young Turks seized power in Istanbul and declared a general amnesty for political and religious prisoners. Between 1911 and 1913 'Abdu'l-Bahá made two extended journeys to bring the faith to the attention of people in North America, Great Britain, France, Germany and Hungary. He spoke at public meetings, social reform associations, churches and synagogues. His approach was typically uncompromising on matters of principle: in Washington, D.C., for example, he scandalized his hosts by insisting that a leading black Bahá'í should sit next to him at a prestigious dinner. Throughout his travels he attracted the attention of the Western media and received a constant flow of visitors of all nationalities, creeds and social positions, including ambassadors, princes, government ministers, academics and leaders of social movements, among them Emmeline Pankhurst, Alexander Graham Bell, Andrew Carnegie, W. E. B. Du Bois and Theodore Roosevelt (*opposite*).

The writer and artist Kahlil Gibran met 'Abdu'l-Bahá on several occasions, and described him in a letter to his friend Mary Haskell:

He is a very great man. He is complete. There are worlds in his soul. And, oh what a remarkable face – what a beautiful face – so real and so sweet ... I have seen the Unseen, and been filled.

'Abdu'l-Bahá's writings, together with the works of the Báb and Bahá'u'lláh, comprise the faith's holy texts. He wrote three books, hundreds of prayers and many letters to Bahá'í communities and various other groups. Notes were taken at some of his talks, and these have been compiled in such volumes as *Paris Talks* and *Some Answered Questions*. The latter includes informal discussions on the relationship between the Bahá'í Faith and Christianity. 'Abdu'l-Bahá returned to the Holy Land in 1913, just before the

above 'Abdu'l-Bahá as a young man.

left Andrew Carnegie, Alexander Graham Bell, Emmeline Pankhurst, and Theodore Roosevelt all met 'Abdu'l-Bahá.

start of the First World War, during which he helped to prevent a local famine in Haifa by feeding the poor with grain he had stored. In 1920 he was knighted by the British government for his humanitarian work, but he never used the title. When he died in 1921 obituaries appeared in newspapers around the world. *The Times* of London, for example, wrote:

He was a man of great spiritual power and commanding presence, and his name was held in reverence throughout the Middle East. He claimed that the revelation given by his father, Bahá'u'lláh, expressed the essential truth of all the religions of the world. He advocated universal peace and brotherhood, the independent investigation of truth, and the equality of the sexes, and frequently made earnest appeals to the rulers of Europe for universal disarmament.

He appointed Shoghi Effendi as his successor in his *Will and Testament*. There are few universal Bahá'í symbols, but 'Abdu'l-Bahá's portrait is one of the faith's most widely recognized images.

above 'Abdu'l-Bahá in later life, as drawn by Kahlil Gibran.

above left Munirih Khanum, the wife of 'Abdu'l-Bahá.

above right Akka from the sea. 'Abdu'l-Bahá acted as Bahá'u'lláh's deputy and secretary in the Akka area for several decades and succeeded him as head of the Bahá'í Faith in 1892.

left 'Abdu'l-Bahá's home in Haifa, where he lived after his release from house arrest in Akka in 1908.

bottom left 'Abdu'l-Bahá at the Eiffel Tower. During two extended journeys to several West European countries in 1911 and 1913 'Abdu'l-Bahá gave a number of public lectures: his talks in Paris, Europe's oldest Bahá'í community, were transcribed and later published under the title *Paris Talks*.

above 'Abdu'l-Bahá was knighted by the British government in 1920 in recognition of his work for famine relief in Palestine during the First World War.

left By the time of his passing in 1921, which was marked by a funeral in Haifa attended by ten thousand people, 'Abdu'l-Bahá had completed the first stage in the construction of the Shrine of the Báb and had written his *Will and Testament* in which he appointed Shoghi Effendi his successor.

Shoghi Effendi

Shoghi Effendi succeeded 'Abdu'l-Bahá, his grandfather, as head of the Bahá'í Faith in 1921, and continued in that capacity until his own death in 1957. As he and his wife had no children and he did not appoint a successor, Shoghi Effendi was the faith's first and only 'guardian' in a projected line of hereditary leaders. His personality, directives and writings shaped the faith's organization and activities during much of the twentieth century. His greatest influences relate to the translation and interpretation in English of a large volume of sacred texts, the strengthening of the faith's world centre in Israel, the launching of plans to spread the religion, and the building up of the Bahá'í system of organization.

Shoghi Effendi's upbringing and education were an unusual blend of East and West, which enabled him to bridge the two cultures. His early years were spent in Palestine as 'Abdu'l-Bahá's secretary and translator. He later studied political economy at Balliol College, University of Oxford, at which time, at the age of twenty-four, he was informed that he had been appointed to lead the Bahá'í Faith. 'Abdu'l-Bahá's *Will and Testament* designated Shoghi Effendi as his successor and described him as 'the expounder of the words of God', 'the chosen branch, the guardian of the Cause of God', and 'the sacred bough that hath branched out from the Twin Holy Trees'. This last passage is a reference to his descent both from the family of the Báb (through his father) and from Bahá'u'lláh (through his mother). Within a year of assuming office, Shoghi Effendi invited Bahá'ís from around the world to Haifa for discussions on the future of the faith. At this meeting it became clear that the Universal House of Justice, the faith's future international council, could not be established until further local and national councils (called 'assemblies') were formed.

right Shoghi Effendi as a young man hiking in Switzerland with a local guide.

Before 1921 very few Bahá'í texts existed in Western languages. One of Shoghi Effendi's priorities was the translation of major works into English. By 1931 he had translated Bahá'u'lláh's *Hidden Words*, a collection of ethical aphorisms, and the *Book of Certitude*, a doctrinal work, as well as *Nabil's Narrative*, an early history of the faith. Shoghi Effendi's own writings usually took the form of long letters addressed to Bahá'í communities. Seven of these letters, written between 1929 and 1936, have been collected under the title of *World Order of Bahá'u'lláh*, a work that explains the Bahá'í vision of international order. In 1944 Shoghi Effendi completed *God Passes By*, a centennial review of Bahá'í history. He also wrote some 26,000 letters in answer to individuals and Bahá'í assemblies. His interpretations of scripture, unlike the writings of the Báb, Bahá'u'lláh and 'Abdu'l-Bahá, are not regarded as sacred texts, but are considered authoritative.

Shoghi Effendi once referred to the Bahá'í World Centre in Israel as the 'heart and nerve-centre of a world faith'. He set the design for the major gardens and buildings and promoted good relations with local and international leaders. He increased the area of property under Bahá'í ownership in the Holy Land fifty-fold. The remains of the Báb had been removed from Iran years earlier, but by 1953, within a space of six years, Shoghi Effendi had transformed the Shrine of the Báb from what he called in 1947 'a homely building with a fortress-like appearance' into the 'Queen of [Mount] Carmel' – a building that to this day attracts many visitors. He met local leaders, such as Israel's Prime Minister, David Ben Gurion, in 1949 and President Ben Zvi in 1954, and also maintained links with international organizations, especially the United Nations.

Bahá'u'lláh was the architect of the system of elected councils that

left Shoghi Effendi designed the gardens surrounding the Shrine of Bahá'u'lláh in Bahji, near Akka.

right Queen Marie of Romania, who corresponded with Shoghi Effendi and wrote many letters and newspaper articles in support of the Bahá'í Faith in the 1920s.

below Facsimile of Her Majesty's written testimonials to the significance of the Bahá'í teachings.

The Bahai teaching brings peace and understanding.

It is like a wide embrace gathering together all those who have long searched for words of hope.

It accepts all great prophets gone before, it destroys no other creeds and leaves all doors open.

Saddened by the continual strife amongst believers of many confessions and wearied of their intolerance towards each other, I discovered in the Bahai teaching the real spirit of Christ so often denied and misunderstood:

Unity instead of strife, Hope instead of condemnation, Love instead of hate, and a great reassurance for all men.

Marie.

Bahá'ís refer to as their 'administrative order' (see pp. 97–112), but it was Shoghi Effendi who supervised and planned its construction. He detailed the powers and processes for the annual election of local and national assemblies, called for the setting up of Bahá'í funds, and instituted advisers called 'Auxiliary Board Members'. He established the International Bahá'í Council, the forerunner of the Universal House of Justice, in 1951 and also appointed more than twenty-five individuals to the most senior advisory position of the Bahá'í Faith, 'Hand of the Cause of God'. Shoghi Effendi saw an efficient system of organization as essential for the foundation and smooth running of a worldwide community. In 1921 there were Bahá'ís in only thirty-five countries, none of which had national Bahá'í assemblies, but by the time of his death in 1957 there were Bahá'ís in 254 countries or territories and twenty-six national or regional assemblies.

History may remember Shoghi Effendi as something of an organizational genius. He avoided the limelight and played down his own personality, but he was held in great esteem and affection. He died suddenly in London, of a heart attack, at the age of sixty, but the community he had built was sufficiently strong to withstand his loss. He was survived by his wife, the late Madame Rabbani, who was among the Hands who led the faith until the election of the Universal House of Justice in 1963.

above Madame Rabbani, widow of Shoghi Effendi, who died in 2000.

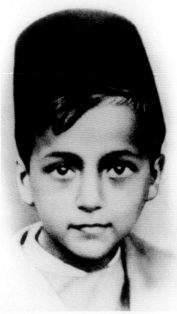

far left The house in Akka where Shoghi Effendi was born on 1 March 1897.

left Shoghi Effendi as a boy.

below Shoghi Effendi with a prominent early Scottish Bahá'í, Dr John Esslemont, who later served as his secretary in Haifa.

above Shoghi Effendi with other students at Balliol College, University of Oxford. His studies were cut short by the passing of his grandfather, 'Abdu'l-Bahá, whom he succeeded as head of the Bahá'í Faith.

right Shoghi Effendi's resting place in London.

SHOGHI EFFENDI ON THE BAHÁ'Í VISION OF WORLD ORDER

Diversity

It [the Bahá'í Faith] does not ignore, nor does it attempt to suppress, the diversity of ethnical origins, of climate, of history, of language and tradition, of thought and habit, that differentiate the peoples and nations of the world. It calls for a wider loyalty, for a larger aspiration than any that has animated the human race. It insists upon the subordination of national impulses and interests to the imperative claims of a unified world. It repudiates excessive centralization on one hand, and disclaims all attempts at uniformity on the other. Its watchword is unity in diversity.

Freedom

The unity of the human race, as envisaged by Bahá'u'lláh, implies the establishment of a world commonwealth in which all nations, races, creeds and classes are closely and permanently united ... in which the autonomy of its state members and the personal freedom and initiative of the individuals that compose them are definitely and completely safeguarded.

Progress of civilization

Bahá'u'lláh's mission is to proclaim that the ages of the infancy and of the childhood of the human race are past, that the convulsions associated with the present stage of its adolescence are slowly and painfully preparing it to attain the stage of manhood, and are heralding the approach of that Age of Ages when swords will be beaten into plowshares.

World citizenship

Though loyal to their respective governments, though imbued with the love of their own country, and anxious to promote at all times its best interests, the followers of the Bahá'í Faith, nevertheless, viewing mankind as one entity, and profoundly attached to its vital interests, will not hesitate to subordinate every particular interest, be it personal, regional or national, to the overriding interests of the generality of mankind, knowing full well that in a world of interdependent peoples and nations the advantage of the part is best to be reached by the advantage of the whole.

BAHÁ'Í HOLY TEXTS comprise the writings of Bahá'u'lláh, the Báb, and 'Abdu'l-Bahá. Bahá'u'lláh, whose writings are most central to the religion, wrote in Persian and in Arabic over a period of forty years, from 1852 to 1892. Over fifteen thousand texts have been collected at the Bahá'í World Centre in Haifa, Israel, comprising about a hundred volumes. In most cases Bahá'u'lláh either wrote with his own hand or dictated his writings to secretaries, checked their transcriptions and used his personal seal to confirm their accuracy. Bahá'u'lláh's writings involve varied styles, two languages and different approaches to truth, addressing a range of rational, mystical, ethical and legal issues. This variety reflects the Bahá'í view that truth is, in some ways, relative. Reality can be appreciated from many perspectives, and any single approach can convey only limited aspects of the whole truth.

sacred texts

main picture 'Bird of Paradise', a tribute to Bahá'u'lláh by eminent nineteenth-century calligrapher Mishkin-Qalam.

left Award-winning cover of a recent edition of Bahá'u'lláh's *Hidden Words*, a collection of ethical reflections.

Major texts In 1858 Bahá'u'lláh composed the *Hidden Words* (described on the opposite page). His next major book was the *Book of Certitude* (1862). Whereas the *Hidden Words* expresses in a fresh way the spiritual message common to all religions, the *Book of Certitude* reveals new aspects of his religion. The latter describes, for example, the process of divine revelation, the nature of divinity and the role of prophets. In effect, it establishes the theological basis of Bahá'í belief. A few years later Bahá'u'lláh wrote a series of letters to several reigning monarchs and religious leaders (see p. 66). In these writings he claimed prophethood, challenged these leaders to investigate his claims, and urged them to establish democracies and just governments and to disarm. This was followed by the *Most Holy Book*. In this work he elaborated on his previous writings on government and social order, revealed specific laws, outlined a system of institutions for the Bahá'í community as well as for wider society, and established a model for Bahá'í law-making. One of Bahá'u'lláh's last major works was the *Book of the Covenant*, a short piece written entirely in his own hand that constitutes his will and testament. Here he explicitly appointed 'Abdu'l-Bahá as his successor as head of the Bahá'í Faith.

below The arrival of the *Most Holy Book* in Papua New Guinea.

Ethical and mystical writings

In 1858, while an exile in Ottoman Iraq, Bahá'u'lláh wrote the *Hidden Words* as he paced the banks of the river Tigris. This work, which draws on the spiritual teachings of past religions 'clothed in the garment of brevity', is one of Bahá'u'lláh's best-loved writings, and has been translated into more than a hundred languages.

Its poetic statements are in no particular sequence, but the book is unified by the theme of the relationship between belief and action, between declared intention and daily behaviour: 'Let deeds not words be your adorning' is Bahá'u'lláh's m`essage. The work builds on a series of statements that exhort those on the path of spirituality to 'give forth goodly and wondrous deeds'. He states: 'Every one must show forth deeds that are pure and holy, for words are the property of all alike.' This work ends with a challenge: 'Let it now be seen what your endeavours in the path of detachment will reveal.' The *Hidden Words* also explores the eternal relationship between God and humanity, the nature of spirituality, and virtues to strive for.

above Pope John Paul II receiving a copy of the *Hidden Words*.

PASSAGES FROM BAHÁ'U'LLÁH'S *HIDDEN WORDS*

Hear no evil, and see no evil, abase not thyself, neither sigh and weep. Speak no evil, that thou mayest not hear it spoken unto thee, and magnify not the faults of others that thine own faults may not appear great; and wish not the abasement of anyone, that thine own abasement be not exposed. Live then the days of thy life, that are less than a fleeting moment, with thy mind stainless, thy heart unsullied, thy thoughts pure, and thy nature sanctified, so that, free and content, thou mayest put away this mortal frame, and repair unto the mystic paradise and abide in the eternal kingdom for evermore.

I created thee rich, why dost thou bring thyself down to poverty? Noble I made thee, wherewith dost thou abase thyself? Out of the essence of knowledge I gave thee being, why seekest thou enlightenment from anyone besides Me? Out of the clay of love I moulded thee, how dost thou busy thyself with another? Turn thy sight unto thyself, that thou mayest find Me standing within thee, mighty, powerful and self-subsisting.

Know thou of a truth: He that biddeth men be just and himself committeth iniquity is not of Me, even though he bear My name.

Verily I say unto thee: Of all men the most negligent is he that disputeth idly and seeketh to advance himself over his brother. Say, O brethren! Let deeds, not words, be your adorning.

Abandon not the everlasting beauty for a beauty that must die, and set not your affections on this mortal world of dust.

Holy words and pure and goodly deeds ascend unto the heaven of celestial glory. Strive that your deeds may be cleansed from the dust of self and hypocrisy and find favour at the court of glory; for ere long the assayers of mankind shall, in the holy presence of the Adored One, accept naught but absolute virtue and deeds of stainless purity. This is the daystar of wisdom and of divine mystery that hath shone above the horizon of the divine will. Blessed are they that turn thereunto.

Bahá'u'lláh's best-known mystical work is the *Seven Valleys* (1857). It was written in response to questions put to him by a Sufi, an Islamic mystic. Bahá'u'lláh employs the form and language of mysticism to describe the seven 'valleys' that represent successive stages of an individual's spiritual journey. Again, Bahá'u'lláh dwells on how the mystical aspects of belief should be expressed in the improvement of the individual's character and in social action. This emphasis on the practical is the most distinguishing feature of Bahá'í mysticism. Throughout the *Seven Valleys* Bahá'u'lláh subtly returns to two themes: the need for the individual to gain access to spiritual ascent through a spiritual luminary or prophet, and the obligation of the enlightened individual to better the world. The ecstasy of 'mystic reunion' is not enough. The seeker must make spiritual progress as well as contribute to society. Parables are used in the *Seven Valleys* to help illustrate these themes. The story of the archetypal lovers, Layli and Majnun, describes the qualities of a truth-seeker: passion, resolve and tenacity. In another parable the seeker is pursued in the night by what he believes to be an angel of death, which actually turns out to be an angel of mercy. True knowledge, the story suggests, is to see the end in the beginning, to perceive divine justice behind life's injustices.

Major writings of Bahá'u'lláh

Title	Description	Approximate date of completion
Seven Valleys	Mystical reflections	1857
Hidden Words	Ethical aphorisms	1858
Book of Certitude	Theological interpretations	1862
Letters to monarchs and rulers	Social and political treatises	1868
Most Holy Book	System of social order and laws	1873
Book of the Covenant	Will and testament	1891

Theological writings

The *Book of Certitude* is the most important doctrinal or theological work by Bahá'u'lláh. He bases this work on a series of structured arguments; his aim is to use logic to instil in the reader a sense of certainty or 'certitude' about religious truth. The work begins with a central question: if God sends spiritual luminaries to educate humanity, why are those prophets, at least initially, rejected and persecuted? Bahá'u'lláh's answer is twofold. First, fantastic expectations come from literal rather than symbolic interpretation of prophecy and scripture. Literal-mindedness is partly the fault of religious leaders who have selfish reasons for rejecting any new faith. Second, most people mistakenly regard their prophet as the last and final prophet of all time.

Two features in the *Book of Certitude* are of special interest to Christians and Muslims. The first is that Bahá'u'lláh, who was writing in an Islamic culture, champions the authenticity of the Bible. He refutes a common Muslim charge that the Bible is a corrupted document, although he says that it has at times been misinterpreted. He says of the Gospels: 'The words of the verses themselves eloquently testify to the truth that they are of God.' He further states that a just God would not cut off that scriptural link between Himself and Christians by allowing corruption of the Gospels. In later works Bahá'u'lláh further develops this theme and affirms the historical truth of the Gospels' accounts of Jesus' crucifixion.

A second feature of interest in the *Book of Certitude* relates to Bahá'u'lláh's description of the two different stations of prophethood. These stations are 'the physical, pertaining to the world of matter' and 'the spiritual, which is born of the substance of God Himself'. For each station, Bahá'u'lláh explains, the prophet uses a different type of language. On some occasions the language of a sacred text describes the prophet's station of 'absolute servitude, utter destitution and complete self-effacement'. At other times the prophet speaks with the authority of the 'Godhead, Divinity, Supreme Singleness'.

The possession of two stations, of two natures, might explain how Jesus could state: 'He who has seen me has seen the Father' and also 'My Father is greater than I' (John 14:9; 14:28). Similarly, Bahá'u'lláh wrote: 'When I contemplate, O my God, the relationship that bindeth me to Thee, I am moved to proclaim to all created things "Verily I am God!"; and when I consider my own self, lo, I find it coarser than clay!'

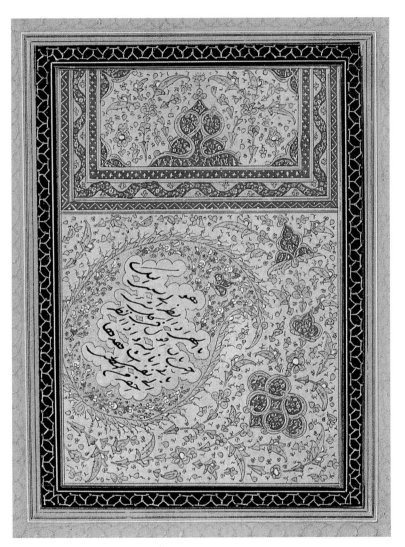

left Illuminated tablet in the handwriting of Bahá'u'lláh. It translates as follows: 'When I contemplate, O my God, the relationship that bindeth me to Thee I am moved to proclaim to all created things, "Verily, I am God!"; and when I consider my own self, lo, I find it coarser than clay!'

QUOTATIONS FROM THE *BOOK OF CERTITUDE*

On religious search

They that tread the path of faith, they that thirst for the wine of certitude, must cleanse themselves of all that is earthly – their ears from idle talk, their minds from vain imaginings, their hearts from worldly affections, their eyes from that which perisheth.

He [the seeker] must never seek to exalt himself above any one, must wash away from the tablet of his heart every trace of pride and vainglory, must cling unto patience and resignation, observe silence and refrain from idle talk. For the tongue is a smouldering fire, and excess of speech a deadly poison . . . He should be content with little, and be freed from all inordinate desire . . . He should forgive the sinful, and never despise his low estate, for none knoweth what his own end shall be.

On God

To every discerning and illumined heart it is evident that God, the unknowable Essence, the divine Being, is immensely exalted beyond every human attribute, such as corporeal existence, ascent and descent, egress and regress. Far be it from His glory that human tongue should adequately recount His praise, or that human heart comprehend His fathomless mystery. He is and hath ever been veiled in the ancient eternity of His Essence, and will remain in His Reality everlastingly hidden from the sight of men ... No tie of direct intercourse can possibly bind Him to His creatures. He standeth exalted beyond and above all separation and union, all proximity and remoteness. No sign can indicate His presence or His absence; inasmuch as by a word of His command all that are in heaven and on earth have come to exist, and by His wish, which is the Primal Will itself, all have stepped out of utter nothingness into the realm of being, the world of the visible.

On Messengers of God

These Prophets and chosen Ones of God are the recipients and revealers of all the unchangeable attributes and names of God. They are the mirrors that truly and faithfully reflect the light of God. Whatsoever is applicable to them is in reality applicable to God, Himself, Who is both the Visible and the Invisible. The knowledge of

Him, Who is the Origin of all things [i.e. God], and attainment unto Him, are impossible save throughknowledge of, and attainment unto, these luminous Beings who proceed from the Sun of Truth. By attaining, therefore, to the presence of these holy Luminaries, the 'Presence of God' Himself is attained. From their knowledge, the knowledge of God is revealed, and from the light of their countenance, the splendour of the Face of God is made manifest.

We have already in the foregoing pages assigned two stations unto each of the Luminaries arising from the Daysprings of eternal holiness. One of these stations, the station of essential unity ... The other is the station of distinction, and pertaineth to the world of creation and to the limitations thereof. In this respect, each Manifestation of God hath a distinct individuality, a definitely prescribed mission, a predestined Revelation, and specially designated limitations. Each one of them is known by a different name, is characterized by a special attribute, fulfils a definite Mission, and is entrusted with a particular Revelation.

On human beings

How resplendent the luminaries of knowledge that shine in an atom, and how vast the oceans of wisdom that surge within a drop! To a supreme degree is this true of man, who, among all created things, hath been invested with the robe of such gifts, and hath been singled out for the glory of such distinction. For in him are potentially revealed all the attributes and names of God to a degree that no other created being hath excelled or surpassed. All these names and attributes are applicable to him.

On scripture

It is evident unto thee that the Birds of Heaven and Doves of Eternity [i.e. the prophets] speak a twofold language. One language, the outward language, is devoid of allusions, is unconcealed and unveiled; that it may be a guiding lamp and a beaconing light whereby wayfarers may attain the heights of holiness, and seekers may advance into the realm of eternal reunion. Such are the unveiled traditions and the evident verses already mentioned. The other language is veiled and concealed, so that whatever lieth hidden in the heart of the malevolent may be made manifest and their innermost being be disclosed.

Social and political works From the mid-1860s

Bahá'u'lláh wrote a series of letters to the world's major rulers. In addition to his claims of prophethood, he described specific programmes of national and international reform aimed at preventing war and at promoting parliamentary government that were regarded as radical. He declared that it was the duty of the state to care for the poor and to provide them with essential services. He linked this teaching to the need for a form of world governance. Global political union based on the principle of collective security would allow smaller military budgets, thereby freeing resources to promote social welfare.

Starting in 1867 Bahá'u'lláh wrote letters to Napoleon III, Queen Victoria, Tsar Alexander II, Pope Pius IX, Emperor Franz Joseph, Kaiser Wilhelm I, Sultan Abdul-Aziz, Nasir-Din Shah and collectively to the leaders of America. A major theme of his writings to Muslim rulers was the separation of religion and state, of obedience by Bahá'ís to the law of the land and of their abstention from violence. In the *Tablet to the Kings* Bahá'u'lláh criticized Sultan Abdul-Aziz of the Ottoman Empire for allowing his subjects to live in squalor while his officials enjoyed an opulent lifestyle. In his writings to the Shah of Iran Bahá'u'lláh urged him to give ordinary people a voice in government.

Bahá'u'lláh singled out Queen Victoria for praise on two counts. He commended the British government for the abolition of slavery, which was still widely practised in the Middle East. He also congratulated her on having 'entrusted the reins of counsel into the hands of the people', a possible reference to the British Reform Act of 1867, which gave more citizens the vote. In this letter Bahá'u'lláh also called for a system of collective security – for all nations to unite and arise against any aggressor nation. He described the increasing military spending in the build-up to the Franco-Prussian War as 'a heinous wrong'. Money that was spent on war deprived the poor of their right to food, shelter and education.

Bahá'u'lláh's second message to Napoleon III and his message to Kaiser Wilhelm I of Germany were less complimentary. Napoleon, for example, had ignored Bahá'u'lláh's first letter, including his request that the French government should pressure the Ottomans to cease persecution of Bahá'ís. Bahá'u'lláh anticipated Napoleon's fall from power: 'For what thou hast done, thy kingdom shall be thrown into confusion, and thine empire shall pass from thy hands, as a punishment for what thou hast wrought.' In these letters Bahá'u'lláh generally reserved praise for constitutional monarchies and for republics, two forms of government of which he approved. By contrast he criticized undemocratic states for injustice, arbitrariness and extremes of wealth and poverty.

Letters to world leaders

Be united, O kings of the earth, for thereby will the tempest of discord be stilled amongst you, and your peoples find rest, if ye be of them that comprehend. Should anyone among you take up arms against another, rise ye all against him, for this is naught but manifest justice.

Kaiser Wilhelm I of Prussia
'Be vigilant, that ye may not do injustice to anyone, be it to the extent of a grain of mustard seed. Tread ye the path of justice, for this, verily, is the straight path. Compose your differences, and reduce your armaments, that the hearts may be tranquilized. Heal the dissensions that divide you, and ye will no longer be in need of any armaments except what the protection of your cities and territories demandeth. Fear ye God, and take heed not to outstrip the bounds of moderation, and be numbered among the extravagant. We have learned that you are increasing your outlay every year, and are laying the burden thereof on your subjects. This, verily, is more than they can bear, and is a grievous injustice.'

Emperor Franz Joseph of Austria
'O kings of the earth! We see you increasing every year your expenditures, and laying the burden thereof on your subjects. This, verily, is wholly and grossly unjust. Fear the sighs and tears of this Wronged One, and lay not excessive burdens on your peoples. Do not rob them to rear palaces for yourselves; nay, rather choose for them that which ye choose for yourselves ... Your people are your treasures.'

Tsar Alexander II of Russia
'Know ye that the poor are the trust of God in your midst. Watch that ye betray not His trust, that ye deal not unjustly with them and that ye walk not in the ways of the treacherous. Ye will most certainly be called upon to answer for His trust on the day when the Balance of Justice shall be set, the day when unto everyone shall be rendered his due, when the doings of all men, be they rich or poor, shall be weighed.'

Nasir-Din Shah of Iran
'O King! I was but a man like others, asleep upon My couch, when lo, the breezes of the All-Glorious were wafted over Me, and taught Me the knowledge of all that hath been. This thing is not from Me, but from One Who is Almighty and All-Knowing. And He bade Me lift up My voice between earth and heaven, and for this there befell Me what hath caused the tears of every man of understanding to flow. The learning current amongst men I studied not; their schools I entered not. Ask of the city wherein I dwelt, that thou mayest be well assured that I am not of them who speak falsely.'

Napoleon III of France

'Exultest thou over the treasures thou dost possess, knowing they shall perish? Rejoicest thou in that thou rulest a span of earth, when the whole world, in the estimation of the people of Bahá [i.e. Bahá'ís], is worth as much as the black in the eye of a dead ant? Abandon it unto such as have set their affections upon it, and turn thou unto Him Who is the Desire of the world. Whither are gone the proud and their palaces? Gaze thou into their tombs, that thou mayest profit by this example, inasmuch as We made it a lesson unto every beholder. Were the breezes of Revelation to seize thee, thou wouldst flee the world and turn unto the Kingdom, and wouldst expend all thou possessest, that thou mayest draw nigh unto this sublime Vision.'

Queen Victoria of Britain

'We have also heard that thou hadst entrusted the reins of counsel into the hands of the representatives of the people. Thou, indeed, hast done well, for thereby the foundations of the edifice of thine affairs will be strengthened, and the hearts of all that are beneath thy shadow, whether high or low, will be tranquilized. It behooveth them, however, to be trustworthy among His servants, and to regard themselves as the representatives of all that dwell on earth.'

Sultan Abdul-Aziz of the Ottoman Empire

'Overstep not the bounds of moderation, and deal justly with them that serve thee. Bestow upon them according to their needs, and not to the extent that will enable them to lay up riches for themselves, to deck their persons, to embellish their homes, to acquire the things that are of no benefit unto them, and to be numbered with the extravagant. Deal with them with undeviating justice, so that none among them may either suffer want, or be pampered with luxuries. This is but manifest justice. Allow not the abject to rule over and dominate them who are noble and worthy of honour, and suffer not the high-minded to be at the mercy of the contemptible and worthless.'

Pope Pius IX

'Call thou to remembrance Him Who was the Spirit [Jesus], Who, when He came, the most learned of His age pronounced judgment against Him in His own country, whilst he [Peter] who was only a fisherman believed in him. Take heed, then, ye men of understanding heart! Thou, in truth, art one of the suns of the heaven and of His names. Guard thyself, lest darkness spread its veils over thee, and fold thee away from his light ... Consider those who opposed the Son [Jesus], when He came unto them with sovereignty and power. How many the Pharisees who were waiting to behold Him, and were lamenting over their separation from Him! And yet, when the fragrance of His coming was wafted over them, and His beauty was unveiled, they turned aside from Him and disputed with Him ... None save a very few, who were destitute of any power amongst men, turned towards His face. And yet today every man endowed with power and invested with sovereignty prideth himself on His Name!'

The writings of the Báb and 'Abdu'l-Bahá

Bahá'ís regard the Báb as both a prophet and the forerunner of Bahá'u'lláh, and his writings are viewed as sacred. His literary output was vast: within three years of claiming prophethood, it is estimated that he had composed some half-million verses. Most of these writings, however, were destroyed in the latter half of the nineteenth century as a result of increasing persecution.

Among the surviving early writings of the Báb, the majority focus on the proclamation of his authority and the arrival of a new religious day, the best known being a commentary on the Koran's Surih of Joseph, revealed when the Báb first declared his mission. The Báb subsequently announced his prophethood in letters to various political and religious leaders of the day, including the Shah, his chief minister, and senior clerics – as Bahá'u'lláh also did several decades later. The Báb's major later work, *The Exposition*, clearly signaled that he had founded a new religion based on a new set of religious laws.

Bahá'ís regard 'Abdu'l-Bahá's writings (and authentic transcriptions of his talks) as holy texts by virtue of his role as the interpreter of Bahá'u'lláh's teachings, even though, unlike the Báb and Bahá'u'lláh, he was not a messenger of God. 'Abdu'l-Bahá wrote on many subjects, including interpretations of Christian doctrine and issues current in Europe and North America such as the emancipation of women, industrial relations, and the harmony between science and religion. His book, *The Secret of Divine Civilization*, published in Iran in 1875, advocated the use of Western methods and technology to help modernize Iran. Over 27,000 of his letters have survived. A theme that runs through many of 'Abdu'l-Bahá's writings is the irresistible trend towards social progress:

All created things have their degree or stage of maturity. The period of maturity in the life of a tree is the time of its fruit-bearing ... The animal attains a stage of full growth and completeness, and in the human kingdom man reaches his maturity when the light of his intelligence attains its greatest power and development ... Similarly there are periods and stages in the collective life of humanity. At one time it was passing through its stage of childhood, at another its period of youth, but now it has entered its long-predicted phase of maturity, the evidences of which are everywhere apparent ... That which was applicable to human needs during the early history of the race can neither meet nor satisfy the demands of this day, this period of newness and consummation. Humanity has emerged from its former state of limitation and preliminary training. Man must now become imbued with new virtues and powers, new moral standards, new capacities. New bounties, perfect bestowals, are awaiting and already descending upon him. The gifts and blessings of the period of youth, although timely and sufficient during the adolescence of mankind, are now incapable of meeting the requirements of its maturity.

IN BAHÁ'Í SCRIPTURES God is described as a universal, supreme being, far removed from the world, utterly unknowable and forever hidden. Prophets are those who link God to humanity, and teach moral and spiritual principles, thereby inspiring new civilizations. All prophets, including Jesus, Buddha and Bahá'u'lláh, are regarded as teaching essentially the same religion and sharing the same spiritual status and purpose.

god and prophets

main picture Dome of the Rock, Jerusalem, with the Western Wall in the foreground, symbols of Israel's multifaith heritage.

left Israeli stamp commemorating the completion of the Bahá'í buildings in Haifa.

above and opposite Religious images from around the world. Bahá'ís believe that all great religions have been inspired by the same source.

God

Bahá'ís believe in one God, described as the creator of the universe, an unknowable essence beyond the understanding of human beings: 'Exalted, immeasurably exalted, art Thou above the strivings of mortal man to unravel Thy mystery, to describe Thy glory, or even hint at the nature of Thine Essence.' Yet Bahá'í writings also describe a personal, loving, compassionate Ultimate Reality that intervenes periodically in history by sending messengers or prophets who act as intermediaries between humanity and the spiritual realm. Bahá'ís believe that people can only know God through these prophets. Just as stainless mirrors can reflect the light of the sun, so these prophets reflect God's qualities in their writings and lives. This makes God unknowable but not remote. Nearness to God is through nearness to His prophets.

Bahá'ís do not believe that Bahá'u'lláh or any other individual could ever be 'God made flesh'. Bahá'í writings also reject the idea that God is merely the sum of the universe. Another Bahá'í belief about God relates to the Bahá'í principle that religious truth is relative and not absolute. This means that all statements and imagery about God are limited by the background, mentality and level of spiritual awareness of the person making the observation. Even so, Bahá'í sacred writings are full of references to God and His qualities. Most Bahá'í prayers celebrate God's perfections, referring, for example, to the All-Powerful, the All-Compassionate, the All-Wise. These qualities are potentially human, and by concentrating upon them in worshipping God, the intention is for people to develop their own spiritual potential.

Common patterns in the lives of prophets

Bahá'u'lláh claimed to be a universal messiah: for example, the return of Christ for Christians and for Muslims. In the *Book of Certitude*, however, he says that the 'return' spoken of in prophecy is not meant as the literal physical return, but as the renewal of a common message and purpose. For example, the major religions share ethical teachings summarized as the 'Golden Rule' (see p. 80).

opposite and below Prayer and a devotional attitude are common features in the world's religions.

It is clear and evident to thee that all the Prophets are the Temples of the Cause of God, Who have appeared clothed in divers attire ... Thou wilt behold them all abiding in the same tabernacle, soaring in the same heaven, seated upon the same throne, uttering the same speech and proclaiming the same faith. Such is the unity of those Essences of being, those Luminaries of infinite and immeasurable splendour. Wherefore, should one of these Manifestations of Holiness proclaim saying: 'I am the return of all the Prophets,' He verily speaketh the truth. (BAHÁ'U'LLÁH)

Bahá'ís refer to common features in the lives of the major religious figures to support this idea. Mystical experiences, for example, marked the start of the careers of several prophets. For Moses it was the episode of the burning bush. In the case of Buddha it was his enlightenment under the Bodhi tree. For Jesus it was the descent of the spirit of God in the form of a dove after his baptism by John. The angel Gabriel appeared to Muhammad near a mountain. For Bahá'u'lláh it was the image of a maiden, seen while he was first imprisoned. After these moments of spiritual insight, however, several prophets experienced periods of struggle, and felt the need for solitude. Jesus spent forty days in the desert. Buddha struggled with Mara, the personification of evil. Bahá'u'lláh lived as a recluse for two years in the mountains of Kurdistan.

Eventually, however, the prophets began to preach, usually first to a small group of devoted followers, then to a wider audience. Jesus gathered twelve apostles. Buddha's first followers were a small group of monks. Bahá'u'lláh's first claim to prophethood was made privately in the company of a select group. Several prophets were initially regarded merely as reformers. With time, however, a clear break was made with the old religion, and the laws and teachings of a new religion were established. Other parallels can be drawn in relation to the ways they made their claims to rulers of their time; faced opposition and subsequent exile; and promised future saviours. Bahá'u'lláh, for example, promised that another prophet would follow him after at least a thousand years.

There are obvious limitations to such sketchy comparisons: there are also wide variations in the lives of the prophets. At least for Bahá'ís, however, such broad similarities support their belief in the unity of prophets:

They only differ in the intensity of their revelation and the comparative potency of their light ... if thou callest them all by one name, and dost ascribe to them the same attribute, thou hast not erred from the truth.
(BAHÁ'U'LLÁH)

above Delegates at the 1924 Conference of Living Religions within the British Empire, attending a reception hosted by Lady Blomfield, a well-known Bahá'í.

Dialogue between religions

Bahá'ís believe that the world's major religions share certain essential features, notwithstanding their differences. They regard these major religions as inspired by the same source: 'Unequivocally and without the least reservation [the Bahá'í Faith] proclaims all established religions to be divine in origin' (*Shoghi Effendi*). The pursuit of religious harmony, Bahá'ís believe, begins with this understanding, that all religions share a common origin. Like the members of a family, religions may differ in age and in character, but their core features unite them across time and cultures.

Bahá'ís start with the premise that all religions share the aim of encouraging good deeds and promoting tolerance, compassion, mercy and justice. They each have a version of the 'Golden Rule', that people should treat others as they themselves would like to be treated. In this sense each new faith is merely a renewal of all previous religions, 'the changeless Faith of God, eternal in the past, eternal in the future' (*Bahá'u'lláh*). Bahá'ís, however, do not ignore their differences. Some of the differences can be explained by each religion's early cultural context (such as dietary restrictions) and the community's degree of social development (such as differences in the status of women). Other differences often stem from scriptural interpretation, misplaced loyalty to clergy or just fanaticism, the enemy of religious harmony. Such fanaticism is condemned in the Bahá'í writings:

Religious fanaticism and hatred are a world-devouring fire, whose violence none can quench ... That the divers communions of the earth, and the manifold systems of religious belief, should never be allowed to foster the feelings of animosity among men, is, in this Day, of the essence of the Faith of God and His Religion.
(BAHÁ'U'LLÁH)

Bahá'u'lláh repeatedly called on his followers to 'consort' with people of other faiths in a spirit of harmony and friendship. Such associations might be expressed in several ways. Bahá'í communities have tried to collaborate with other religious groups in projects that aim to relieve human suffering. In addition to forging links based on such ethical concerns, 'Abdu'l-Bahá encouraged Bahá'ís to experience the religious life of other traditions and to share worship and meditation. Another approach is intellectual. By identifying differences and similarities among religions Bahá'ís believe that scholars might see the religious traditions of the world as part of one progressive process. The Bahá'í call for dialogue also applies to religious leaders, whom the international governing council of the Bahá'í Faith has urged:

[Renounce] all those claims to exclusivity or finality that, in winding their roots around the life of the spirit, have been the greatest single factor in suffocating impulses to unity and in promoting hatred and violence. It is to this historic challenge that we believe leaders of religion must respond if religious leadership is to have meaning in the global society emerging from the transformative experiences of the twentieth century. It is evident that growing numbers of people are coming to realize that the truth underlying all religions is in its essence one. This recognition arises not through a resolution of theological disputes, but as an intuitive awareness born from the ever widening experience of others and from a dawning acceptance of the oneness of the human family itself. Out of the welter of religious doctrines, rituals and legal codes inherited from vanished worlds, there is emerging a sense that spiritual life, like the oneness manifest in diverse nationalities, races and cultures, constitutes one unbounded reality equally accessible to everyone.
(UNIVERSAL HOUSE OF JUSTICE, 2002)

The Golden Rule

Tsekung asked, 'Is there one word that can serve as a principle of conduct for life?' Confucius replied, 'It is the word shu – reciprocity: Do not do to others what you do not want them to do to you.'

Confucianism: ANALECTS 15:23

That nature only is good when it shall not do unto another whatever is not good for its own self.

Zoroastrianism: DADISTAN-I-DINIK

One going to take a pointed stick to poke a baby bird should first try it on himself to feel how it hurts.

YORUBA PROVERB, NIGERIA

Regard your neighbour's gain as your own gain and your neighbour's loss as your own loss.

Taoism: T'AI SHANG KAN YING P'IEN

Never do to others what would pain thyself.

Hinduism: PANCHATANTRA 3:104

Not one of you is a believer until he loves for his brother what he loves for himself.

Islam: FORTY HADITH OF AN-NAWAWI 13

Treat others as thou wouldst be treated thyself.

Sikhism: ADI GRANTH

You shall love your neighbour as yourself.

Judaism: LEVITICUS 19:18

Desire not for anyone the things that ye would not desire for yourselves.
Bahá'í Faith: GLEANINGS 66

All things whatsoever ye would that men should do to you, do ye even so to them: for this is the law and the prophets.
Christianity: MATTHEW 7:12

Hurt not others with that which pains yourself. Buddhism: UDANA 5:18

THE PURPOSE OF RELIGION

Is not the object of every Revelation to effect a transformation in the whole character of mankind, a transformation that shall manifest itself both outwardly and inwardly, that shall affect both its inner life and external conditions? For if the character of mankind be not changed, the futility of God's universal Manifestations would be apparent. (BAHÁ'U'LLÁH)

The cause of this fellowship and unity lies in the fact that the divine law has two distinct aspects or functions: one the essential or fundamental, the other the material or accidental. The first aspect of the revealed religion of God is that which concerns the ethical development and spiritual progress of mankind, the awakening of potential human susceptibilities and the descent of divine bestowals. These ordinances are changeless, essential, eternal. The second function of the divine religion deals with material conditions, the laws of human intercourse and social regulation. These are subject to change and transformation in accordance with the time, place and conditions. The essential ordinances of religion were the same during the time of Abraham, the day of Moses and the cycle of Jesus, but the accidental or material laws were abrogated and superseded according to the exigency and requirement of each succeeding age. ('ABDU'L-BAHÁ)

The Revelation, of which Bahá'u'lláh is the source and centre, abrogates none of the religions that have preceded it, nor does it attempt, in the slightest degree, to distort their features or to belittle their value. It disclaims any intention of dwarfing any of the Prophets of the past, or of whittling down the eternal verity of their teachings. It can, in no wise, conflict with the spirit that animates their claims, nor does it seek to undermine the basis of any man's allegiance to their cause. Its declared, its primary purpose is to enable every adherent of these Faiths to obtain a fuller understanding of the religion with which he stands identified, and to acquire a clearer apprehension of its purpose. It is neither eclectic in the presentation of its truths, nor arrogant in the affirmation of its claims. Its teachings revolve around the fundamental principle that religious truth is not absolute but relative, that Divine Revelation is progressive, not final. Unequivocally and without the least reservation it proclaims all established religions to be divine in origin, identical in their aims, complementary in their functions, continuous in their purpose, indispensable in their value to mankind. (SHOGHI EFFENDI)

body, mind and spirit

BAHÁ'Í SCRIPTURES TEACH that the human body is a temporary home for the development of an eternal soul. Nevertheless, it should be treated with care, both to prevent human suffering and out of respect for its close association with the soul. Bahá'í teachings discourage smoking and forbid the use of alcohol and mind-altering drugs. Bahá'ís value rational thought, and regard the mind as the essential quality of the soul. They also practice the classical spiritual disciplines of daily meditation, prayer and, for a few weeks each year, fasting.

main picture Bahá'í houses of worship are open to all people for meditation and prayer.

left One of the fountains beautifying the terraces leading up Mount Carmel to the Shrine of the Báb, a place of pilgrimage for Bahá'ís.

Tobacco, alcohol and drugs

Tobacco, alcohol and drugs For Bahá'ís, smoking tobacco is strongly discouraged as an unhealthy addiction, but it is not forbidden. Alcohol, opiates, cannabis and other mind-altering drugs are, by contrast, forbidden, unless they are prescribed for medical reasons.

The drinking of wine [and other alcoholic beverages] is, according to the text of the Most Holy Book, forbidden; for it is the cause of chronic diseases, weakeneth the nerves ... and causeth man to commit acts of absurdity. ('ABDU'L-BAHÁ)

Opium fasteneth on the soul, so that the user's conscience dieth, his mind blotted away, his perceptions are eroded. It turneth the living into the dead. ('ABDU'L-BAHÁ)

Bahá'í teachings on addictive substances generally reflect the importance placed on good physical health for individuals, but they also seek to promote healthy communities by reducing social ills associated with drug and alcohol abuse, such as crime, violence and poverty. Also, by avoiding 'mind-altering' drugs, the individual can maintain moral and spiritual responsibility for his or her actions, whereas this may be lost during intoxication with substances, such as heroin, that cause 'the disintegration of thought and the complete torpor of the soul' *('Abdu'l-Bahá)*.

Health, healing and diet

Bahá'í texts regard human illness as chiefly a biological problem. According to 'Abdu'l-Bahá, the principal causes of disease are physical and Bahá'ís are encouraged to seek the best available medical advice when they become ill. In the *Most Holy Book* Bahá'u'lláh writes: 'Should ye be attacked by illness or disease, consult skilful physicians.' Individuals should take medicines that are prescribed by doctors, but should avoid becoming dependent on them. The practice of medicine itself is highly praised: '[It] is the most important of all the sciences for it is the greatest means ... for preserving the bodies of all people' *('Abdu'l-Bahá)*. Despite the emphasis on seeking medical treatments for illness, Bahá'ís also believe that prayer may have a beneficial effect.

Apart from advice on smoking, alcohol and drugs, Bahá'í texts make a few general comments on healthy living. Physical cleanliness is important. Vegetarianism is encouraged: 'Abdu'l-Bahá anticipated that fruits and grains would be the foods of the future. But the keys to balanced living are common sense and moderation:

A good character is, in the sight of God and His chosen ones and the possessors of insight, the most excellent and praiseworthy of all things, but always on condition that its centre of emanation should be reason and knowledge, and its base should be true moderation. ('ABDU'L-BAHÁ)

Reason Bahá'u'lláh said that reason is God's greatest gift to the soul, 'a sign of the revelation of the sovereign Lord'. The act of questioning is encouraged as a means of developing faith, rather than being seen as a threat to religious belief. Faith is defined as 'conscious knowledge', and Bahá'í teachings reject blind belief and imitation. Intellectual investigation is seen as 'the most praiseworthy power' possessed by human beings, their 'most precious gift' *('Abdu'l-Bahá)*.

The 'heart' and the mind should both be devoted to the process of spiritual discovery. Bahá'í teachings also emphasize, however, that there are other ways to approach truth, including aesthetics, intuition and mysticism. As truth is many-sided, no single approach can exhaust it. Bahá'ís believe that this variety of approaches helps them avoid fundamentalist thinking.

above and opposite Bahá'ís believe that spiritual discovery involves reason, prayer, discussion, and reflection.

Spirit Bahá'í writings address fundamental spiritual questions about the nature of the soul, the meaning of life and the afterlife, as described below in the writings of 'Abdu'l-Bahá.

On the human soul
Verily I say, the human soul is, in its essence, one of the signs of God, a mystery among His mysteries. God has created ... man and endowed him with powers of advancement towards spiritual and transcendent heights.

On the soul's progress
Know verily all the souls are created according to the nature of God and all are in the state of purity at the time of their births. But afterward they differ from one another insofar as they acquire excellencies or defects.

*If a man's thought is constantly aspiring towards heavenly subjects then
does he become saintly; if on the other hand his thought does not soar,
but is directed downwards to centre itself upon the things of this world,
he grows more and more material.*

On the purpose of life
*Man is, in reality, a spiritual being, and only when he lives in the spirit is
he truly happy.*

On death
*To consider that after the death of the body the spirit perishes is like
imagining that a bird in a cage will be destroyed if the cage is broken,*

*though the bird has nothing to fear from the destruction of the cage...Our
body is like the cage, and the spirit is like the bird...If the cage becomes
broken, the bird will continue and exist. Its feelings will be even more
powerful, its perceptions greater, and its happiness increase...For the
thankful birds, there is no paradise greater than freedom from the cage.*

*Therefore in this world he [man] must prepare himself for the life
beyond. That which he needs in the world of the Kingdom must be
obtained here...The world beyond is a world of sanctity and radiance;
therefore it is necessary that in this world he should acquire these divine
attributes. In that world there is need of spirituality, faith, assurance, the
knowledge and love of God. These he must attain in this world so that
after his ascension from the earthly to the heavenly Kingdom he shall find
all that is needful in that life eternal waiting for him. By what means can
man acquire these things? How shall he obtain these merciful gifts and
powers? First, through the knowledge of God. Second, through the love of
God. Third, through faith. Fourth, through philanthropic deeds. Fifth,*

through self-sacrifice. Sixth, through severance from this world. Seventh, through sanctity and holiness.

Someone asked: 'How should one look forward to death?'

The answer: 'How does one look forward to the end of any journey? With hope and with expectation.'

On the afterlife

The world beyond is as different from this world as this world is different from that of the child while still in the womb of its mother.

The difference and distinction between men will naturally become realized after their departure from this mortal world. But this distinction is not in respect to place, but in respect to the soul and conscience. For the Kingdom of God is sanctified (or free) from time and place; it is another world and another universe. As to the soul of man after death, it remains in the degree of purity to which it has evolved during life in the physical body, and after it is freed from the body it remains plunged in the ocean of God's mercy.

The rewards of the other world are peace, the spiritual graces, the various spiritual gifts in the Kingdom of God, the gaining of the desires of the heart and soul, and the meeting of God in the world of eternity. In the same way the punishments of the other world, that is to say, the torments of the other world, consist in being deprived of the special divine blessings and the absolute bounties, and falling into the lowest degrees of existence.

The wealth of the other world is nearness to God ... The rich in the other world can help the poor, as the rich can help the poor here. In every world, all are the creatures of God. They are always dependent on Him.

Know thou of a truth that if the soul of man hath walked in the ways of God, it will assuredly return and be gathered to the glory of the Beloved. By the righteousness of God! It shall attain such a station as no pen can depict, or tongue describe. The soul that hath remained faithful to the Cause of God, and stood unwaveringly firm in His path, shall, after his ascension, be possessed of such power that all the worlds which the Almighty hath created can benefit through him.

A number of beautiful souls passed beyond this earthly life. Although such an event is indeed regrettable, we must realize that everything which happens is due to some wisdom and that nothing happens without a reason. Therein is a mystery; but whatever the reason and mystery, it was a very sad occurrence, one which brought tears to many eyes and distress to many souls. I ['Abdu'l-Bahá] was greatly affected by this disaster. Some of those who were lost voyaged on the Cedric with us as far as Naples and afterward sailed upon the other ship. When I think of them, I am very sad indeed. But when I consider this calamity in another aspect, I am consoled by the realization that the worlds of God are infinite; that though they were deprived of this existence, they have other opportunities in the life beyond, even as Christ has said, 'In my Father's house are many mansions'. They were called away from the temporary and transferred to the eternal; they abandoned this material existence and entered the portals of the spiritual world. Forgoing the pleasures and comforts of the earthly, they now partake of a joy and happiness far more abiding and real, for they have hastened to the Kingdom of God. The mercy of God is infinite, and it is our duty to remember these departed souls in our prayers and supplications that they may draw nearer and nearer to the Source itself.

These human conditions may be likened to the matrix of the mother from which a child is to be born into the spacious outer world. At first the infant finds it very difficult to reconcile itself to its new existence. It cries as if not wishing to be separated from its narrow abode and imagining that life is restricted to that limited space. It is reluctant to leave its home, but nature forces it into this world. Having come into its new conditions, it finds that it has passed from darkness into a sphere of radiance; from gloomy and restricted surroundings it has been transferred to a spacious and delightful environment. Its nourishment was the blood of the mother; now it finds delicious food to enjoy. Its new life is filled with brightness and beauty; it looks with wonder and delight upon the mountains, meadows and fields of green, the rivers and fountains, the wonderful stars; it breathes the life-quickening atmosphere; and then it praises God for its release from the confinement of its former condition and attainment to the freedom of a new realm. This analogy expresses the relation of the temporal world to the life hereafter – the transition of the soul of man from darkness and uncertainty to the light and reality of the eternal Kingdom. At first it is very difficult to welcome death, but after attaining its new condition the soul is grateful, for it has been released from the bondage of the limited to enjoy the liberties of the unlimited. It has been freed from a world of sorrow, grief and trials to live in a world of unending bliss and joy. The phenomenal and physical have been abandoned in order that it may attain the opportunities of the ideal and spiritual. Therefore, the souls of those who have passed away from earth and completed their span of mortal pilgrimage in the Titanic disaster have hastened to a world superior to this. They have soared away from these conditions of darkness and dim vision into the realm of light. These are the only considerations which can comfort and console those whom they have left behind.

Meditation, fasting and prayer

Meditation, fasting, prayer and the daily reading of scripture are the main Bahá'í spiritual disciplines, and are regarded as ways of promoting spiritual growth. They are obligatory, but their performance is left entirely to the conscience of the individual. No particular pattern of meditation is suggested, so Bahá'ís are free to use any method they find comfortable. To assist their reflection, Bahá'ís often read passages from scripture, with an emphasis on developing one's understanding of spiritual truths rather than blind recital: 'One hour's reflection is preferable to seventy years of pious worship' (*Bahá'u'lláh*). In keeping with this link between spirituality and action, Bahá'u'lláh asks Bahá'ís to review their actions at the end of each day as part of a process of self-development.

Fasting is common to many traditions. In early Christianity Lent was a forty-day period of fasting; in Judaism there is a twenty-four-hour fast on Yom Kippur; and Ramadan is the annual Islamic month of fasting. Bahá'ís fast for nineteen days each year, from 2 to 20 March. During this time they do not eat or drink from sunrise to sunset. This is regarded as a period of spiritual regeneration, and of reflection on one's spiritual progress. Fasting is essentially a symbol of detachment from material things: 'For this material fast is an outer token of the spiritual fast; it is a symbol of self-restraint, the withholding of oneself from all appetites of the self, taking on the characteristics of the spirit' (*'Abdu'l-Bahá*). Fasting is meant to remind Bahá'ís of the suffering of the poor, to bring families and communities together in a common endeavour, to strengthen the resolve of individuals and to help individuals rededicate themselves to the spiritual life. People aged under fifteen or over seventy, pregnant and nursing women, the sick and those engaged in heavy work are exempt from fasting.

Private prayer is part of the individual's daily spiritual life. The aim of prayer is to give the individual 'life to his soul and exultation to his being' (*'Abdu'l-Bahá*). The spiritual state induced by prayer is more important than the physical act. Bahá'u'lláh stressed that brief and joyful prayer is preferable to long but wearying worship. Certain prayers are specified for daily practice to instil humility, devotion and spiritual discipline. In addition, Bahá'u'lláh and 'Abdu'l-Bahá provided many prayers for general use, as well as for special occasions (such as the Bahá'í New Year), and at times of difficulty. The use of revealed prayers enables the reader to meditate freely on the ideas contained in the verses, rather than trying to find the right words to communicate suitable thoughts and feelings, making the activity of prayer an experience of remembrance. Most prayers written by Bahá'u'lláh do not have to be said in any special way. They can be read quietly or chanted aloud, sung, or otherwise adapted to various cultures and individual preferences. Bahá'í devotional meetings may combine prayer, reflection and music in an uplifting ambience. Prayers play an integral part in most Bahá'í gatherings, but there are no prayer leaders.

MEDITATION

*While you meditate you are speaking with your own spirit. In that
state of mind you put certain questions to your spirit and the spirit
answers: the light breaks forth and the reality is revealed ...*

*Through the faculty of meditation man attains to eternal life;
through it he receives the breath of the Holy Spirit – the bestowal of
the Spirit is given in reflection and meditation. The spirit of man is
itself informed and strengthened during meditation; through it affairs
of which man knew nothing are unfolded before his view. Through it
he receives Divine inspiration, through it he receives heavenly food.*

*Meditation is the key for opening the doors of mysteries. In that
state man abstracts himself: in that state man withdraws himself
from all outside objects; in that subjective mood he is immersed in
the ocean of spiritual life and can unfold the secrets of things-in-
themselves. To illustrate this, think of man as endowed with two
kinds of sight; when the power of insight is being used the outward
power of vision does not see. This faculty of meditation frees man
from the animal nature, discerns the reality of things, puts man in
touch with God.*

*This faculty brings forth from the invisible plane the sciences
and arts. Through the meditative faculty inventions are made
possible, colossal undertakings are carried out; through it
governments can run smoothly. Through this faculty man enters into
the very Kingdom of God. Nevertheless some thoughts are useless to
man; they are like waves moving in the sea without result. But if the
faculty of meditation is bathed in the inner light and characterized
with divine attributes, the results will be confirmed.*

*The meditative faculty is akin to the mirror; if you put it before
earthly objects it will reflect them. Therefore if the spirit of man is
contemplating earthly subjects he will be informed of these. But if
you turn the mirror of your spirits heavenwards, the heavenly
constellations and the rays of the Sun of Reality will be reflected in
your hearts, and the virtues of the Kingdom will be obtained.*

*Therefore let us keep this faculty rightly directed – turning it to
the heavenly Sun and not to earthly objects – so that we may
discover the secrets of the Kingdom, and comprehend the allegories
of the Bible and the mysteries of the spirit.*

May we indeed become mirrors reflecting the heavenly realities,
and may we become so pure as to reflect the stars of heaven.

('ABDU'L-BAHÁ)

BAHÁ'Í PRAYERS

Short obligatory prayer

I bear witness, O my God, that Thou hast created me to know Thee and to worship Thee.

I testify at this moment to my powerlessness and to Thy might, to my poverty and to Thy wealth.

There is none other God but Thee, the Help in Peril, the Self-Subsisting.

(BAHÁ'U'LLÁH)

Prayer for spiritual growth

From the sweet-scented streams of Thine eternity give me to drink, O my God, and of the fruits of the tree of Thy being enable me to taste, O my Hope!

From the crystal springs of Thy love suffer me to quaff, O my Glory, and beneath the shadow of Thine everlasting providence let me abide, O my Light!

Within the meadows of Thy nearness, before Thy presence, make me able to roam, O my Beloved, and at the right hand of the throne of Thy mercy, seat me, O my Desire!

From the fragrant breezes of Thy joy let a breath pass over me, O my Goal, and into the heights of the paradise of Thy reality let me gain admission, O my Adored One!

To the melodies of the dove of Thy oneness suffer me to hearken, O Resplendent One, and through the spirit of Thy power and Thy might quicken me, O my Provider!

In the spirit of Thy love keep me steadfast, O my Succourer, and in the path of Thy good-pleasure set firm my steps, O my Maker!

Within the garden of Thine immortality, before Thy countenance, let me abide for ever, O Thou Who art merciful unto me, and upon the seat of Thy glory stablish me, O Thou Who art my Possessor!

To the heaven of Thy loving-kindness lift me up, O my Quickener, and unto the Day-Star of Thy guidance lead me, O Thou my Attractor!

Before the revelations of Thine invisible spirit summon me to be present, O Thou Who art my Origin and my Highest Wish, and unto the essence of the fragrance of Thy beauty, which Thou wilt manifest, cause me to return, O Thou Who art my God!

Potent art Thou to do what pleaseth Thee. Thou art, verily, the Most Exalted, the All-Glorious, the All-Highest.

(BAHÁ'U'LLÁH)

community life and organization

BAHÁ'Í COMMUNITY LIFE is organized around local activities such as the 'feast' (a regular community gathering), study circles, devotional meetings, children's classes, and regional meetings such as conventions and seminars. Institutions at local, regional, and international levels assist in the organization of these and other activities.

Bahá'í institutions share certain goals: collective responsibility for the success of any enterprise; involvement by the vast majority of the membership or 'universal participation'; and open debate and discussion in decision-making, a process called 'consultation'.

main picture Bahá'í mother and child in Papua New Guinea.

left Stamp showing the Samoan house of worship, around which community and charitable organizations are anticipated to develop.

Marriage, family life and children

Bahá'ís are encouraged to marry, to raise children, and to live as families. The family is regarded as a community's central institution. 'Abdu'l-Bahá suggested that the social progress of a community is associated with the well-being of its families:

Compare the nations of the world to the members of a family. A family is a nation in miniature. Simply enlarge the circle of the household and you have the nation. Enlarge the circle of nations and you have all humanity.

('ABDU'L-BAHÁ)

above and opposite Bahá'í teachings emphasize the importance and sanctity of marriage and family life.

Family life helps the individual to develop various qualities such as generosity, love, co-operation and patience. Marriage, in particular, provides the individual with a 'fortress for well-being'. As described below, Bahá'í teachings on marriage and family life involve a combination of apparently different values, some of which might be seen today as traditional and others as progressive.

Bahá'í writings describe marriage as an 'attachment of mind and heart' or 'a union of the body and of the spirit' (*'Abdu'l-Bahá*). The goal of married people is to become 'two helpmates', 'two intimate friends', 'even as a single soul' (*'Abdu'l-Bahá*). Marriage should therefore be based on spiritual bonds as well as physical attraction: 'If the marriage is based both on the spirit and the body, that union is a true one, hence it will endure' (*'Abdu'l-Bahá*). Bahá'í teachings state that sex should take place only between people married to each other. According to Shoghi Effendi, 'the proper use of the sex instinct is the natural right of every individual, and it is precisely for this very purpose that the institution of marriage has been established. Bahá'ís do not believe in the suppression of the sex impulse, but in its regulation and control.'

Bahá'ís are permitted to marry from the age of fifteen, subject to the laws of the country in which they live. At any age, however, Bahá'í law requires that the couple's parents agree to the marriage before it takes place. Bahá'ís can marry people from any other religious and cultural background, and the practice of arranged marriages is discouraged. Bahá'í marriage ceremonies can be very simple. Apart from the exchange of a short vow – 'We will all, verily, abide by the will of God' – the couple is free to arrange the ceremony as they wish. Divorce is permitted, but only as a last resort, and on

completion of a 'year of patience', in which the couple spends at least one year apart attempting to reconcile: 'Truly, the Lord loveth union and harmony and abhorreth separation and divorce' (*Bahá'u'lláh*).

Harmonious Bahá'í family life involves a balance of rights and responsibilities. Children, for example, have a duty to obey their parents. They also have the right to be cared for, educated and protected. Although the Bahá'í writings suggest that the mother is 'the first educator of the child' (*'Abdu'l-Bahá)*, this is intended to be applied flexibly: responsibility for the education of children rests with both parents. As Bahá'ís believe that one of the most important functions of marriage is to raise children who will become useful members of society, the performance of that task is regarded as worship:

Know ye that in God's sight, the best of all ways to worship Him is to educate the children and train them in all the perfections of humankind; and no nobler deed than this can be imagined. (BAHÁ'U'LLÁH)

Community gatherings and holy days

Bahá'ís regularly gather as local communities for several types of meetings. The most important is called the 'feast', which is a monthly community gathering for prayer, discussion and fellowship. Bahá'ís also come together to celebrate their 'holy days'. There are nine major days during the year, which commemorate special historical events. There is also a trend for local Bahá'í communities to host devotional meetings that anyone can attend to reflect, pray and socialize together. At the national level Bahá'ís may gather for thematic conferences, residential schools and retreats, and various seminars. Most countries hold annual conventions, where the national governing bodies are elected by secret ballot.

The nineteen-day feast

The Bahá'í calendar consists of nineteen months, each comprising nineteen days (19 x 19 = 361 days), plus four or five additional 'intercalary' days to complete the calendar. The nineteen-day feast is the focal gathering of each local Bahá'í community, generally held on the first day of each Bahá'í month. It has three parts: the devotional, the practical and the social. The first involves reading prayers and meditations from scripture, which are usually from Bahá'í texts but can also be taken from the sacred writings of other religions. The second part is a general meeting where the local assembly shares news and messages from other Bahá'í communities, and reports on its own activities, plans and problems. This part involves discussion of ideas, suggestions and criticisms – a process called 'consultation' (see panel opposite). The third part of the feast involves taking refreshments together and socializing.

Simplicity and hospitality are key features of the feast. Despite its name, Bahá'u'lláh explains that a feast should be held even if only water can be served. Individuals or groups of individuals usually prepare feasts. Most are held in people's homes, some in larger properties rented or owned by Bahá'ís, and others in the open air. The feast's simple outline and lack of ritual allows it to be adapted to different cultural and social settings, and feasts in many Bahá'í communities are evolving to reflect the distinctive characteristics of the societies in which they are held. The wider context of the feast is also important. It is a meeting in which the basic elements of community life – acts of worship, festivity and other forms of fellowship – come together. The feast is also a link between the individual and the wider Bahá'í world, and it is intended to 'educate its participants in the essentials of responsible citizenship' (*Universal House of Justice*).

above Bahá'í gatherings usually involve fellowship and socializing, but their form varies from culture to culture.

opposite Members of the National Spiritual Assembly of Ecuador in consultation.

DECISION-MAKING IN BAHÁ'Í COMMUNITIES

'Consultation' is a process of collective decision-making prescribed in Bahá'í writings and used by Bahá'í assemblies, committees and other groups. Its aim is to provide an opportunity for the free exchange of ideas and to assist in solving problems by fostering an attitude of cooperation and truth seeking among participants.

Objectives

Solve problems

•

Make plans

•

Brainstorming

•

Create ownership and enthusiasm by sharing responsibility
for decision-making and planning

Principles

Ascertain facts, identify issues, clarify relevant principles,
find solutions and test them

•

Opinions and ideas are contributions to the group and belong to it,
rather than to the proposer

•

Frank and open expression of views:
'The shining spark of truth comes after the clash of
differing opinions'
('ABDU'L-BAHÁ)

•

Harmony and cohesion (rather than squabbling and factionalism)

•

Majority voting, but everyone is expected to support the decision

Holy days and other meetings

There is historical significance in the commemoration of each of the nine major Bahá'í holy days (see panel below). Bahá'ís are encouraged not to work on these days, and communities hold commemorative meetings. Such gatherings often include the recounting of relevant histories, music, and prayers and meditations on the day's theme, although there are no prescribed formulas. The Bahá'í New Year celebration, for example, falls on 21 March, the first day of spring in the northern hemisphere. The timing of this festive occasion brings to mind the idea of renewal, applied both to nature and to the spirit. Everyone is welcome to attend holy day activities, festive events, and devotional meetings. In recent years, Bahá'ís have adopted a more systematic approach to the study of their holy texts and of their central beliefs. These gatherings are organized at local levels (often called 'study circles') and are open to Bahá'ís and others.

above and top Festive Bahá'í holidays such as New Year may involve singing or dance performances, picnics and parties, and most holy day commemorations include the sharing of refreshments.

Major Bahá'í holy days	
Naw-Rúz (New Year)	21 March
Ridván – first day	21 April
Ridván – ninth day	29 April
Ridván – twelfth day	2 May
the Báb's declaration of his mission	23 May
passing of Bahá'u'lláh	29 May
martyrdom of the Báb	9 July
birth of the Báb	20 October
birth of Bahá'u'lláh	12 November

Organization

Bahá'í organization involves two parallel arms, elected and appointed, that are complementary to each other. Collectively this system is called the 'administrative order', and its principles were outlined in Bahá'í writings. Its day-to-day purpose is to run the affairs and to implement the teachings of the religion. Its long-term goal, however, is to provide a model of social organization, elements of which might be adopted by wider society.

The elected branch consists of nine-member councils called 'assemblies', or 'spiritual assemblies'. Assemblies operate at both local and national levels, and their functions are meant to be decentralized so that decisions can be made at the lowest appropriate level. By 2007 there were about 180 national and regional assemblies, and about 10,000 local assemblies worldwide. The Universal House of Justice also consists of nine members, and is the supreme authority of the faith (see diagram below).

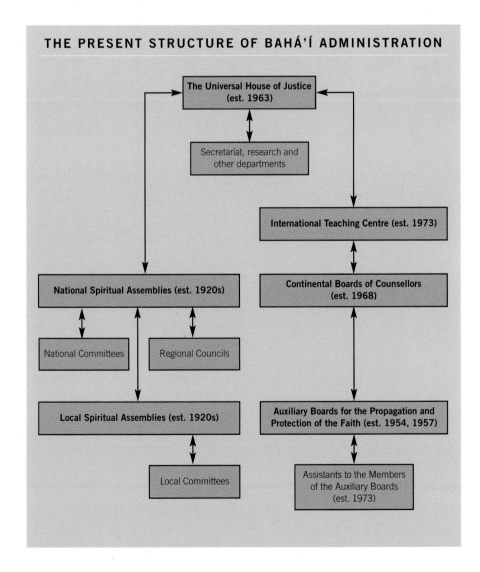

THE PRESENT STRUCTURE OF BAHÁ'Í ADMINISTRATION

- The Universal House of Justice (est. 1963)
- Secretariat, research and other departments
- International Teaching Centre (est. 1973)
- National Spiritual Assemblies (est. 1920s)
- Continental Boards of Counsellors (est. 1968)
- National Committees
- Regional Councils
- Local Spiritual Assemblies (est. 1920s)
- Auxiliary Boards for the Propagation and Protection of the Faith (est. 1954, 1957)
- Local Committees
- Assistants to the Members of the Auxiliary Boards (est. 1973)

Three features of the assembly system stand out. The first is that power resides with the institutions rather than with the individuals serving on them. Assembly members do not act like clergy or have any special privileges. This is intended to reduce the opportunity for corruption or attempts by individuals to concentrate power. A second feature is the lack of nominations, electioneering and political groupings. All adult Bahá'ís of good standing over the age of twenty-one are eligible to serve on assemblies and to vote in annual local elections. National and international elections involve voting by delegates chosen to represent their local communities. All of these elections involve secret ballots. Electors are encouraged to select individuals with wisdom, experience, intellectual ability, dedication and altruism. Local and national elections occur annually; international elections occur every five years. A third feature is the emphasis in assemblies on collective decision-making. As mentioned earlier, Bahá'ís refer to this process as 'consultation'.

In practice, local assemblies meet regularly to discuss community issues, pastoral care and events such as 'feasts' and holy day celebrations. Small-scale projects are often sponsored by local assemblies. Such activities might focus on a particular area of social action, such as the improvement of race relations or the education of children. Communities in Western countries are generally still small enough for most Bahá'ís to have the opportunity to serve on a local assembly at some stage.

above First day of the 1963 Bahá'í World Congress at the Royal Albert Hall, London.

right The 1963 Bahá'í World Congress attracted over 8,000 participants from all over the world.

Whereas assembly members are elected, appointed advisers such as 'Counsellors' and 'Auxiliary Board Members' comprise the complementary arm of the administrative system. Their mandate is to protect and promote the interests of the faith by offering advice, support and inspiration to assemblies, communities and individuals. Their advice is not binding, and individuals appointed as advisers, usually for a term of five years, donate their time and expertise. Like assemblies, advisers function at local, regional, national and international levels. The International Teaching Centre, located at the Bahá'í World Centre, co-ordinates the work of some eighty Counsellors worldwide who liaise with designated national communities. Nearly a thousand Auxiliary Board Members worldwide and their assistants deal chiefly with regional and local matters.

top left and right Every five years Bahá'í delegates, comprising the members of national spiritual assemblies, come from all over the world to participate in the international convention to elect the new members of the Universal House of Justice, and to consult together on the affairs of their faith.

second, third and fourth from top, left Images from the 1992 Bahá'í World Congress, New York, which attracted over 25,000 people from all over the world.

The Bahá'í World Centre

The Bahá'í Faith's leaders continued to work and reside in the Haifa/Akka area (now in Israel) after Bahá'u'lláh's death there in 1892. The Bahá'í places in this area have been developed as a focus for pilgrimage, a place where spiritual significance and outward beauty awaken in Bahá'ís a deeper understanding of their religion. The resting places and shrines of Bahá'u'lláh, the Báb and 'Abdu'l-Bahá are located in this area in the midst of magnificent gardens that are leading local tourist attractions. The administration that oversees the international affairs of the faith is also in Haifa. Collectively these sites are known as the Bahá'í World Centre. As the faith's international headquarters, it coordinates various national offices, proposes international goals and plans, monitors social and economic development projects, compiles statistics, and manages international funds.

Bahá'u'lláh visited Mount Carmel in Haifa on several occasions after his release from confinement. During one of these visits, near the end of his life, he wrote the *Tablet of Carmel* in which he anticipated the construction that would be started by his successors to transform that mountain face. He

marked the spot that was to be the site of the Shrine of the Báb, and by 1909 'Abdu'l-Bahá accomplished the first stage of constructing the shrine, leaving Shoghi Effendi to complete it in 1953.

In the 1940s Shoghi Effendi took two decisions that have influenced the construction on Mount Carmel ever since. The first was to trace a path in the shape of an arc across gardens east of the Shrine of the Báb and immediately above the monuments of the resting-places of Bahá'u'lláh's family members. This path marks sites that are now occupied by the principal administrative buildings of the Bahá'í World Centre. The second decision was to design the International Bahá'í Archives building in a classical Greek style. Shoghi Effendi stated that this architectural style had 'stood the test of time'. This building's completion in 1957 not only provided a place to preserve sacred objects associated with the faith's history, but also established the building style for the remaining buildings on the arc.

The next major phase of development on Mount Carmel occurred in the 1980s and 1990s. The building of the offices of the Universal House of Justice was completed in 1983, and in 1987 construction began on the other administrative buildings. These include an extension to the International Bahá'í Archives building (and, eventually, an international Bahá'í library), a centre for the study of Bahá'í scripture, and a centre that coordinates the work of Bahá'í communities around the world. Nineteen terraces were constructed above and below the Shrine of the Báb, which lead from the bottom to the top of the mountain, embracing the shrine like the ornamental setting of a jewel. These developments have changed a stony mountain face into one of the most attractive spots in the Mediterranean.

above Terraces leading up to the Shrine of the Báb on Mount Carmel.

top left The International Bahá'í Archives building was completed in 1957.

opposite The Seat of the Universal House of Justice on Mount Carmel, Haifa.

Bahá'í World Centre Pilgrimage to these sites of beauty is intended to awaken in Bahá'ís a deeper sense of spiritual significance and understanding of their faith.

Bahá'í funds

Bahá'ís regard generosity as highly virtuous. It includes acts of charity (for example, giving money to the poor, especially during the 'intercalary days' preceding the Bahá'í New Year) and giving to Bahá'í funds. There are funds for local communities, funds to support construction work in Haifa and elsewhere, and many more. For most of these funds the amount given, and the fund to which it is given, are left entirely to the individual. One fund, the 'right of God', is special: individuals are asked to pay nineteen per cent of any income they have which is in excess of their 'necessary' expenses – but they may define for themselves what is 'necessary'. Contributions to these funds are made on a confidential basis and are accepted only from Bahá'ís, and they are used to help achieve the objectives of the religion and to finance its organization. Giving to the funds is regarded as a spiritual obligation akin to prayer and fasting: all Bahá'ís are encouraged to participate, regardless of their level of wealth. Giving to the Bahá'í funds should, however, be tempered by practical considerations. Individuals should not incur debts in order to give to the fund, nor should they forget their other financial obligations.

HOUSES OF WORSHIP ARE SACRED TEMPLES that are open to everyone, Bahá'í or otherwise, as places of prayer and meditation. They are visual symbols of the meeting of cultures and religions under the canopy of a united world. At present there are eight purpose-built houses of worship around the world reflecting distinctive cultural styles. This chapter also covers several Bahá'í's who have produced acclaimed works of art, as Bahá'í writings describe artistic endeavour as a form of worship: 'When thy fingers grasp the paintbrush, it is as if thou wert at prayer in the Temple' (*'Abdu'l-Bahá*).

art and architecture

main picture Bahá'í house of worship in New Delhi, India.

left Pot by Bernard Leach, a celebrated potter who became a Bahá'í in 1940.

Two of the eight houses of worship are located in Australasia, two in Latin America, and one in each of the remaining four continents. All share certain structural features, including a large central dome, nine sides, light-filled centres, and local cultural elements. The interiors are free from elaborate displays (as well as from sermons and prescribed ceremonies). Apart from these features, however, they differ greatly in size, style and architectural merit, as one would expect of eight temples built over several decades in different countries. The Bahá'í writings envisage that such temples will one day be built widely, serving as the spiritual focus of a humanitarian centre that will include a hospital, various schools, an old people's home and an orphanage.

The most celebrated temples are those in New Delhi, India (completed in 1986) and in Illinois, USA (1953). The Indian temple has won several architectural awards and is already a popular tourist attraction (see chart below). Its design is of a nine-petalled lotus flower that appears to float in a series of surrounding pools. The temple's architect seized on the lotus blossom as one of the few unifying decorative symbols common to Hindus, Buddhists and Muslims. The house of worship outside Chicago is the tallest of the Bahá'í temples, designed soon after the pioneering skyscraper constructions began in the nearby city. Its minaret-like towers evoke a mosque, whereas its dome resembles a soaring church.

The other temples are more modest in their designs. The first house of worship was built in Ashkhabad, Turkmenistan (1903), but was later closed down by Soviet authorities and eventually destroyed after an earthquake. In Uganda (1961) the temple's circular shape and flaring eaves resemble an African hut. The shape of the temple in Samoa (1984) evokes the design of fales, or local huts, while the walls of the temple in Panama (1972) are covered with Mayan ornamental patterns. The house of worship in Germany (1964) has the most unusual design, a daring glass and concrete Bauhaus structure.

top Bahá'í house of worship in Ashkhabad, Turkmenistan.

above centre Bahá'í house of worship in Wilmette, near Chicago, USA.

above Bahá'í house of worship in Apia, Samoa.

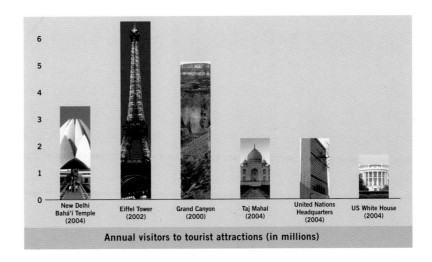

Annual visitors to tourist attractions (in millions)

top left Bahá'í house of worship at Hofheim, near Frankfurt, Germany.

top centre Bahá'í house of worship in Panama.

above Bahá'í houses of worship in Kampala, Uganda (top), near Sydney, Australia (middle), and (bottom) the model of the temple in Chile, currently under construction..

left Bahá'í house of worship in New Delhi, India.

architectural features Bahá'í houses of worship share certain structural features, including a large central dome, nine sides, and light-filled centres. Most evoke elements of local design.

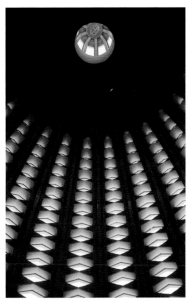

The gardens of the temples help to distinguish the sacred space of worship from everyday life, and evoke the ancient religious imagery of paradise. Fountains, pools and nearby bodies of water call to mind purity, cleanliness and everlasting life. Hilltop sites and domes create symbolic mountains for the faithful to climb. Concentric circles – from the circular walkways of exterior grounds to central domes – represent the central Bahá'í teaching of unity. Perhaps illuminated temples are themselves ultimately physical metaphors for the founders of the world religions.

above The lotus-blossom design of the Bahá'í temple in India is a unifying symbol common to Hindus, Buddhists, and Muslims.

I dreamed
That stone by stone I reared a sacred fane,
A temple, neither Pagod, Mosque nor Church
But loftier, simpler, always open-doored
To every breath from heaven, and Truth
And Love and Justice came and dwelt therein
TENNYSON, AKBAR'S DREAM (1892)

Art and artists

For Bahá'ís, art and spirituality are closely related. Music is a 'ladder by which souls may ascend to the realm on high' *(Bahá'u'lláh)*. 'Treasures lie hidden beneath the throne of God; the key to those treasures is the tongue of poets' *(the Báb)*. This section features the work of several Bahá'ís who have produced acclaimed artwork.

Mark Tobey, a twentieth-century visual artist, is best known for his 'white writing', an energetic derivation of the techniques of Eastern calligraphy. He became a Bahá'í in 1918, and the effects of his religion on his art are often noted. In an essay for Tobey's 1962 retrospective at the Museum of Modern Art in New York, William Sietz wrote: 'Without doubt this [acceptance of the Bahá'í Faith] was the crucial spiritual redirection of Tobey's life and of his development as an artist.' Tobey was the first American painter since Whistler to win the Venice Biennale, and he was given a retrospective at the Louvre in 1961, the first living foreign artist to be so honoured.

opposite Mark Tobey, a major modern
American artist, became a Bahá'í
in 1918.

below *The Last Supper* by Mark Tobey
(Metropolitan Museum of Art).

right Hoop dancing by Kevin Locke, noted Native American artist.

below Sand painting by David Villasenor.

left Potter Bernard Leach.

centre right Bernard Leach's illustration of the Shrine of the Báb.

centre left *Wounded Man* by Reginald Turvey (National Art Gallery of South Africa).

bottom Stamp featuring Bernard Leach pot.

In the 1930s, while teaching art at Dartington Hall in England, Tobey encountered Bernard Leach and Reginald Turvey, a South African painter, both of whom subsequently became Bahá'ís. For Leach, a potter recognized in 1998 by the British Broadcasting Corporation as one of the twentieth century's hundred most important artists, it seemed a natural progression of his desire to fuse the aesthetic and spiritual values of East and West:

Bahá'u'lláh gave warning that the world needs a spiritual core: spirit over matter – not matter over spirit. A spirit with which to release love, understanding and justice, bringing about the maturity of man, an end to war and for the first time, peace on earth. (BERNARD LEACH)

... and all the atoms cry aloud

I bear Him *witness now*
Who by the light of suns beyond the suns beyond
the sun with shrill pen

revealed *renewal of*
the covenant of timelessness with time,
proclaimed
advent of splendor joy

alone can *comprehend*
and the imperious evils of an age could not
withstand and stars

and stones *and seas*
acclaimed – His life its crystal image and
magnetic field.

I bear Him *witness now –*
mystery Whose major clues are the heart of man,
the mystery of God:

Bahá'u'lláh:
Logos, poet, cosmic hero, surgeon, architect
of our hope of peace,

wronged, exiled *One,*
chosen to endure what agonies of knowledge,
what
auroral dark

bestowals of *truth*
vision power anguish for our future's sake.
"I was but a man

"like others, *asleep upon*
My couch, when, lo, the breezes of the All-
Glorious
were wafted over Me ..."

Called, as *in dead of night*
a dreamer is roused to help the helpless flee
a burning house.

I bear Him *witness now:*
toward Him our history in its disastrous quest
for meaning is impelled.

(Angel of Ascent 61–2)

Robert Hayden was the first black American to serve as 'poetry consultant' to the Library of Congress (a position now called Poet Laureate). Hayden refused, however, to be labelled as either a 'black' or a 'Bahá'í' poet; yet few modern poets have written so well from both of these perspectives – as an African-American in a violent society, and as a member of the Bahá'í Faith during its relative obscurity in the West. On his death *Time* magazine said: 'Hayden's work evoked a heroic sense in the black American past.' His work also expressed his spiritual vision:

I think of the writing of poems as one way of coming to grips with inner and outer realities – as a spiritual act, really, a sort of prayer for illumination and perfection. The Bahá'í Faith, with its emphasis on the essential oneness of mankind and its vision of world unity, is an increasingly powerful influence on my poetry today – and the only one to which I willingly submit.

right Poet Robert Hayden.

opposite Jazz musician Dizzy Gillespie.

above American Bahá'í folk music duo, Seals & Croft.

top right Omid Djalili, a Bahá'í actor and comedian, who won *Time Out*'s Best Stand Up Comedian of 2000, first made his mark at the Edinburgh Fringe Festival.

below Rainn Wilson, Bahá'í actor and comedian, and member of the cast of the award-winning U.S. television series *The Office*.

Jazz trumpeter John Birks 'Dizzy' Gillespie, a Bahá'í from 1968 until his death in 1993, helped create the jazz variant called 'be-bop'. His racially diverse 'United Nations Band' broke new ground in fusing Latin American and black American jazz traditions. In his memoirs he wrote: 'Becoming a Bahá'í changed my life in every way and gave me a concept of the relationship between God and man – between man and his fellow man – man and his family. It's just all-consuming. I became more spiritually aware, and when you're spiritually aware, that will be reflected in what you do.'

Lasse Thoresen, on the other hand, is a composer and professor of classical music at the Oslo Music Academy. His Carmel Eulogies, which premiered in 1994, was commissioned by the Oslo Philharmonic Orchestra on the occasion of its seventy-fifth jubilee. The symphony was broadcast on Norwegian radio and television, and consists of a Latin rendition of Bahá'u'lláh's *Tablet of Carmel* (see p. 108). According to Thoresen:

As a Bahá'í and an artist, my ideal is of course to convey some spiritual insight through my music, hopefully without my own ego [getting] too much in the way. To purify the mental sources of inspiration, to open the right channels, so to speak, one has to submit oneself to some spiritual discipline, and the Bahá'í Faith has offered me many means and opportunities to do that. It still does – this process never ends.

Generally, there is great variety in the work of Bahá'í artists: from the calligraphy of Mishkin-Qalam, to the folk songs of Seals and Croft, to the Native American hoop-dancing of Kevin Locke, to the comic acting of Omid Djalili.

contemporary
challenges

SOME OF THE PROBLEMS that face the Bahá'í community, such as the persecution of its Iranian members, are as old as the religion itself. Other challenges, such as attempts to engage in large-scale social action, have become more prominent in recent years. The promotion of racial unity and of the equality of women and men remain major concerns of Bahá'ís.

main picture Slums in New Delhi. Initiating social and economic development projects reflects the Bahá'í commitment to social justice.

left A Bahá'í economic initiative in India to teach marketable skills to promote self-sufficiency in rural areas.

above Destruction of the National Bahá'í Centre, Tehran, in 1955.

Persecutions in Iran

On 20 September 1981 a report in London's *Sunday Times* warned of a 'final solution', in which Iran's third of a million Bahá'ís would suffer a holocaust similar to that of Jews in Nazi Germany. Under Iran's Islamic constitution and laws the Bahá'í religion, unlike Christianity, Judaism and Zoroastrianism, is not recognized. This allows flagrant persecution, since Iranian courts have ruled that Bahá'ís, as 'unprotected infidels', enjoy no rights of redress or protection against assault, killing and torture. In August 1983 Iran's attorney-general formally outlawed any Bahá'í organization.

Fortunately a holocaust has not occurred, but Iran's Bahá'ís have suffered severe persecution. Since the 1979 revolution over two hundred have been killed, hundreds have been imprisoned, and tens of thousands have been made homeless and removed from their jobs. Bahá'í assets, welfare agencies, cemeteries and holy places have been confiscated or destroyed. Bahá'ís were at first barred from all forms of education and Bahá'í teachers dismissed from their jobs. Although school education was reinstated in the late 1980s, university education was not – a decree of the Supreme Revolutionary Council on 25 February 1991 stated: 'The government's dealings with the Bahá'ís must be such that their progress is blocked … they must be expelled from universities, either in the admission process or during the course of their studies, once it becomes known that they are Bahá'ís.' The Iranian Bahá'í community then organized an Open University-style Bahá'í Institute of Higher Education, but in October 1998 thirty-six members of its faculty were arrested, and textbooks, computers and furniture belonging to the school were seized by the government's intelligence agency.

Such persecution is not new. Iran's Bahá'ís have been subject to recurrent attacks for over a century and a half, and perhaps as many as twenty thousand were killed in the pogroms of the 1840s and 1850s. Like Jews in European history, Bahá'ís have been convenient scapegoats during modern Iran's moments of transition and crisis. A theological reason explains this: Bahá'ís from Muslim backgrounds are regarded as apostates because nearly all Muslims believe that divine revelation ended with Muhammad. In addition, Bahá'ís are viewed as morally suspect because they promote the equality of women and men, and because they encourage personal investigation of religious truth (rather than the Shi'ite doctrine of imitating spiritual mentors). Even old Muslim foes have found common cause in persecuting Bahá'ís. In 1845, perhaps for the only time in modern history, leaders of the traditionally antagonistic Shi'ite and Sunni sects of Islam co-produced a legal pronouncement (*fatwa*), in which they publicly condemned the new religion.

During most of the twentieth century the official reasons for killing Bahá'ís were based on charges designed to call into question their patriotism and morality, and Bahá'ís accused of 'spying' or 'prostitution' would have their charges dropped if they recanted their faith. After the Islamic revolution of 1979 accusations such as 'heresy' and 'apostasy from Islam' as well as moral and political charges have been used against Bahá'ís. The political allegations are often contradictory. For example, an article published in 1987 in *Keyhan International*, an official Iranian government newspaper, associates Bahá'ís with Zionism, Western

below left Destruction of the house of the Báb, Shiraz, in 1979.

below right Portrayal of the death of a Bahá'í in 1911.

above Ten Bahá'í women hanged in Shiraz in 1983 for participating in Bahá'í community activities, such as leading children's classes.

imperialism, collaboration with the Saudi Arabian monarchy and with Saddam Hussein – all at the same time.

Publicity of the persecutions has provided much of the Western public's awareness of the religion. Even the first mention in the West was a report in *The Times* of London in 1845 that described the arrest and torture of four early disciples. In 1893 E. G. Browne, a Cambridge orientalist, described how Nasir-Din Shah had lessened his 'horrid cruelties' towards the Bahá'ís because of 'the fear of European public opinion, and desire to be thought well of at Western courts and in Western lands'. The wave of anti-Bahá'í attacks of 1955 was stopped mostly due to pressure from the Eisenhower administration and appeals from the United Nations. It is likely that similar protests from Western media and governments have helped to lessen the most recent outbursts of persecution, and they have certainly brought the plight of Iran's Bahá'ís to the attention of a large segment of the Western public.

These persecutions have also created internal challenges for the Bahá'í community, such as the creation of a large gap in the religion's international finances when contributions from Iran were stopped following the revolution, and the difficulties in integrating several tens of thousands of Bahá'ís who fled Iran to the West during the 1980s and 1990s. The persecutions have, on the other hand, provided the Bahá'í world with a poignant rallying-point and raised its public profile. For the three hundred thousand Bahá'ís who remain in Iran, however, a generation has passed without religious organization. Iranian Bahá'ís, previously renowned for educational and professional excellence, have been forced to the margins of a religious state which denies them higher education, training, work, legal recognition and civil rights.

Campaign for peace
Peace of varying kinds is promised in the Bahá'í writings. The 'lesser peace' involves international political measures to embody the oneness of humanity and prevent war, while the 'greater peace' represents the ultimate aim: the spiritualization of the world community of nations as the foundation for lasting peace. Bahá'ís view the development of their own communities as a peace-making effort – perhaps because these communities are grassroots models of how different people can work together creatively.

'Abdu'l-Bahá wrote letters of encouragement to many peace groups during the first decades of the twentieth century, including the *Tablet to The Hague*, which addressed an international peace conference in the Netherlands in 1919. Few outside the Bahá'í community, however, knew much about Bahá'í views on global peace before the United Nations International Year of Peace in 1986. To mark that occasion the Universal House of Justice addressed a peace message to the people of the world

entitled *The Promise of World Peace*, which has been distributed to at least a million people and to most heads of state. This twenty-five-page message outlines promising features in the current global system, identifies the world's most serious problems, and offers a framework to promote a more just world. Its publication was important to the Bahá'í community, not only because it spelled out positions on issues ranging from nuclear disarmament to market economics, but also because its distribution brought Bahá'ís into contact with many prominent thinkers and leaders. *The Promise of World Peace* illustrates the general approach of Bahá'ís to contemporary problems: deliberately short on exact details, but with an emphasis instead on shifts in attitude needed for lasting change.

Some distinctive aspects of the Bahá'í approach emerge by comparing it with other religious peace messages published to mark the international year of peace, for example from the Pope (1986), the World Council of Churches (1983) and the World Methodist Council (1985). All these messages, for example, say that peace is more than the absence of armed conflict. Apart from the Bahá'í message, however, their proposals deal chiefly with disarmament. By contrast, *The Promise of World Peace* says:

Banning nuclear weapons, prohibiting the use of poison gases, or outlawing germ warfare will not remove the root causes of war. However important such practical measures are as elements of the peace process, they are in themselves too superficial to exert an enduring influence. People are ingenious enough to invent yet other forms of warfare ... A genuine universal framework must be adopted.

above The seven Bahá'í leaders arrested in 2008 whose trial began on 12 January 2010 are, seated from left, Behrouz Tavakkoli and Saeid Rezaie, and, standing, Fariba Kamalabadi, Vahid Tizfahm, Jamaloddin Khanjani, Afif Naeimi, and Mahvash Sabet. The photograph was taken several months before their arrest in Tehran.

This 'universal framework' is described as a decentralized confederation of nations united by a common parliament, an executive, judiciary, security pact, economic system and, perhaps most importantly, awareness of the oneness of humankind. Its message is unashamedly idealistic, described by one commentator as 'responsible utopianism', and described by Johan Galtung, professor of politics at Princeton University, as a plan 'so clear, so commanding that the image itself becomes a live force'.

Another revealing difference relates to the way the different religious bodies view science and technology. The Bahá'í statement is the only one that focuses on the potential good in science:

The scientific and technological advances occurring in this unusually blessed century portend a great surge forward in the social evolution of the planet, and indicate the means by which the practical problems of humanity may be solved. They provide, indeed, the very means for the administration of the complex life of a united world.

Two other Bahá'í documents complement *The Promise of World Peace*. *The Prosperity of Humankind*, published in 1994, outlines the Bahá'í approach to social and economic development (see next section). The other document, *Turning Point for All Nations* (1995), proposes changes to the United Nations on the occasion of that organization's fiftieth anniversary. It supports, for example, wider roles for the General Assembly and the International Court of Justice. These and other Bahá'í efforts towards peace have not gone unnoticed. In 1987 the Bahá'í International Community received a 'Messenger of Peace' award from the United Nations. Various bodies have sought the advice of the Universal House of Justice on peace, and the leaders of a few countries have made personal visits to the Bahá'í World Centre.

Social action
David Jordan, president of Stanford University at the time of 'Abdu'l-Bahá's lecture there in October 1912, described him as treading 'the mystic way' with 'practical feet'. This statement might also reflect the religion's commitment to social reform as well as to spiritual principles. Bahá'í writings state that the purpose of life is to 'work for the betterment of the world' ('*Abdu'l-Bahá*). Bahá'u'lláh encouraged his followers to be involved with pressing contemporary issues: 'Be ye anxiously concerned with the needs of the age ye live in.'

Until recently, however, Bahá'ís were merely advocates rather than practitioners of these ideals. Bahá'í social reforms were impossible to sustain in Iran because of persecution. Before 1960 the involvement of Western Bahá'ís in projects of social change chiefly meant cooperation with groups such as the National Association for the Advancement of Colored People in

above A Bahá'í-run orphanage set up in Tokyo, 1924, following a major earthquake.

America, or with Esperantists in Europe. The situation changed when the religion spread more widely to developing countries, and extreme poverty became a very real part of Bahá'í experience. By 2007 there were more than 500 long-term projects for social and economic development (a substantial number of which are tutorial schools in poor countries), and over 2,500 projects of fixed duration. A substantial number of these projects also relate to health, agriculture and community development. Notable successes have included the establishment of five radio stations in South America that promote indigenous culture as well as mother-and-child health programmes, and a project in rural India that has helped to eradicate Guinea worms in around 300 villages.

Various Bahá'í teachings reflect an underlying concern for social and economic justice. 'Abdu'l-Bahá said that charitable deeds bestow 'honour upon humankind'. Bahá'ís believe in income redistribution through progressive taxation, and the principle of profit-sharing is promoted in Bahá'í writings. Also given strong emphasis is the importance of equality of the sexes, and many Bahá'í community development projects have focused on the empowerment of women in low-income countries. Education is regarded as a universal right, and Iran's Bahá'ís have achieved their country's highest levels of literacy. Despite this commitment to social action, Bahá'ís avoid affiliation with political parties, regarding such partisan action as divisive in nature. Bahá'ís, consequently, may vote for any candidate running in a civic election and can take public positions on purely social or moral issues. They may not, however, identify themselves with, or campaign for, any political party or partisan movement.

Social projects

right Bahá'í-sponsored radio station in Ecuador.

below This Vocational Institute for the Education of Rural Women, Indore, India, is a Bahá'í community project promoting education and financial self-sufficiency for tribal and rural women.

Social action In 2011 there were over 500 long-term projects operated by Bahá'í communities around the world to promote social and economic development. Many of these focus on education, health initiatives, and fostering environmental conservation; others promote rural self-sufficiency. Shown above is a Bahá'í mobile health project in a remote village in Papua New Guinea; the photo top right shows a tree-planting project in India to provide medicinal-grade eucalyptus oil; other images show plumbing and engineering classes (**right, far right**).

Equality between the sexes

The twentieth century saw a worldwide movement towards equality of the sexes, albeit far from complete. But in nineteenth-century Iran such an idea was unthinkable. Bahá'u'lláh's teachings on this subject were therefore challenging: 'Women and men have been and will always be equal in the sight of God.' Human progress will be realized only when 'women and men coordinate and advance equally' ('Abdu'l-Bahá).

Bahá'í teachings on the role of women in the community combine a number of different views, some of which might today be regarded as progressive and others as traditional. The faith, for example, exalts the status of parenthood (and of motherhood in particular) and downgrades the importance of several traditionally male-dominated pursuits, such as military activities. Women are encouraged to pursue careers and family life (if they wish to do so), and their partners are expected to be supportive. If resources are scarce, the education of girls should take priority over the education of

above Lady Sara Louisa Blomfield, a member of London high society and prominent British Bahá'í at the time of 'Abdu'l-Bahá and Shoghi Effendi. She worked tirelessly for the Save the Children Fund and wrote several books on Bahá'í history.

right Lidia Zamenhof, daughter of the Esperanto movement's founder, became a Bahá'í in the 1920s. She was an active Esperantist until her death in Treblinka concentration camp in 1942.

boys because, as mothers, women are believed to be better transmitters of knowledge and skills to future generations. Girls should not be raised as shrinking violets: in the famous Tarbiyat Bahá'í school in Tehran, for example, girls began physical education classes in 1911, fifteen years before they were started in any other Iranian school for girls. Iranian Bahá'í women made particularly impressive progress before the 1979 revolution. By 1973 female Bahá'ís under the age of forty had almost one hundred per cent literacy, compared with an average rate of fifteen per cent in the general female population.

During 'Abdu'l-Bahá's visits to Western Europe and North America in 1911–12, suffragettes warmly embraced Bahá'í teachings on women. Many of the most notable Western Bahá'ís at that time were women, who also comprised a disproportionate number of the faith's public representatives before 1950. The two most important women in Bahá'í history are, however, associated with its early days: Tahirih, a poet and leading disciple of the Báb, and Bahiyyih Khanum, daughter of Bahá'u'lláh. Some regard the charismatic Tahirih as a latter-day Joan of Arc. Like this Christian saint, she was killed while still a young woman, but not before she had publicly unveiled her face in 1848 in a shocking gesture that broke all Islamic mores. Bahiyyih Khanum, by contrast, lived until her eighties and shared the grinding existence of her father's exiles. Her wise, steadying influence was most felt when she acted as head of the faith for nearly a year in the 1920s before Shoghi Effendi assumed full office.

The experience of the Bahá'í community in involving women in positions of leadership varies geographically, but is generally improving over time. Most national communities have task forces that promote women's affairs. Many Baha'i community development projects have focused on the empowerment of women in low-income countries. For example, in Botswana, a sewing club has offered new opportunities for women without jobs. The cooperative, which started in 1995, is based in Oodi, a small village north of the capital. In Afghanistan, a Baha'i-inspired UN programme has sparked the creation of local and regional networks of women who meet regularly, providing a forum to voice opinions and influence local decisions.

In many Middle Eastern countries the election of women to Bahá'í assemblies has marked the first time that women have assumed positions of leadership in those countries. The representation of women on elected national councils varies considerably from region to region: from twenty per cent in Africa to forty-four per cent in Europe. Bahá'í sacred texts do not appear to allow for the possibility of female members of the Universal House of Justice. This apparent anomaly is accepted as a matter of faith, although the writings indicate that it will be clarified in the future.

above Martha Root, distinguished Bahá'í and journalist, travelled widely in the first half of the twentieth century to promote the faith, introducing it to Queen Marie of Romania and Lidia Zamenhof, among others.

MAKE HASTE
by Tahirih

Make haste, the dawn of guidance has begun to breathe
The whole world has been illumined, all the lands and their
peoples

No longer will the shaykh recline on the seat of deception
No more will the mosque be a selling-place for false piety

The turban's chin strap will be cut
No shaykhs, no hypocrisy, no deceit will remain

The world will be freed from illusion and superstition
Humanity will be liberated from all confusion and deception

Oppression will be condemned through the might of equality
Ignorance will be destroyed by the power of perception

In every direction the carpet of equity will be spread
In every direction the seeds of amity will be scattered

The rule of discord will be lifted from all the lands
The root of difference will be transformed into oneness

above Poem by Tahirih, leading disciple
of the Báb, who was killed as a young
woman for her beliefs by the authorities
in Iran.

left Louis and Louisa Gregory.

Racial unity
Few social ills are condemned as strongly in the Bahá'í writings as racism. In a message to the first Universal Races Congress in 1911, 'Abdu'l-Bahá referred to racism as a force that destroys 'the foundations of society' and overthrows 'the banners of life and joy'. Shoghi Effendi identified it as one of the three 'false gods' of twentieth-century thought (the other two being nationalism and communism). *The Promise of World Peace* describes racism as a 'baneful evil'. These uncompromising statements reflect the importance of racial harmony in achieving the central Bahá'í aim of unity.

The American Bahá'í community has been particularly committed to eradicating racial discrimination. America's legacy of slavery, in particular, led Shoghi Effendi to call racism its 'most challenging issue'. The interracial marriage in 1912 of Louis Gregory, a prominent black lawyer from Washington, D.C., and Louisa Matthews, an Englishwoman who studied at the University of Cambridge, was a unifying symbol for the American Bahá'í community. A number of leading black Americans became attracted to the faith, including Alain Locke (see p. 152), Robert Hayden (see p. 124) and Robert Abbott, founder of the *Chicago Defender* newspaper.

The efforts of American Bahá'ís in promoting racial unity inside and outside their own communities have been reasonably successful. In 1937

above Race Amity Conference, Springfield, Maine, 1921, one of many initiatives organized by Bahá'ís to promote racial unity.

Bahá'ís established an annual Race Unity Day, which continues to be celebrated with hundreds of marches, picnics, festivals and conferences. Bahá'ís also participate in the activities of other groups, including the annual Martin Luther King Day parade in Atlanta. King's late widow, Coretta Scott King, said: 'The Bahá'í community ... is always a multi-racial group and I think that is the way Dr King would want us to live.' In 1992 the American national assembly published an open letter in leading newspapers calling for concerted action against a resurgent tide of racism. In 1994 Bahá'ís testified to the Senate foreign relations committee in support of an international convention on the elimination of all forms of racial discrimination.

Expansion

Expansion Bahá'ís are forbidden to engage in aggressive activities to convert people, as this runs counter to the religion's principle of the independent search for truth. Instead, they should share their faith in a dignified and respectful way with those who express interest. The faith has no paid missionaries, but Bahá'ís may wish to 'pioneer' – to leave one's normal place of residence to take the faith to new areas. Partly as a result of such 'pioneering' efforts, the Bahá'í religion has become second only to Christianity in its geographical spread after only 150 years of existence, with Bahá'ís now living in every country and territory apart from the Vatican City. This fact, however, disguises the very thin spread of Bahá'ís in most regions of the world.

Nonetheless, the faith's numerical expansion since the early 1950s has been remarkable. At that time there were only two hundred thousand Bahá'ís (ninety per cent of whom lived in Iran), with perhaps seven hundred local assemblies and twelve national assemblies worldwide. More than forty years later the Bahá'í World Centre reported that there were at least six million Bahá'ís (perhaps a slightly conservative estimate), in excess of 10,000 local assemblies and about 180 national assemblies worldwide.

The largest Bahá'í community in the world is now in India, where large-scale conversions took place mainly in villages during the 1960s and 1970s. In addition to the more than two million Bahá'ís of South Asia, there are at least as many Bahá'ís in the combined registers of the countries in sub-Saharan Africa, Latin America, South-East Asia and Polynesia. Such growth has usually been sparked by systematic campaigns with broad appeal, especially when local Bahá'ís and pioneers have shown that the faith complements various local traditions. Such 'universalism' has attracted people of very different backgrounds – from avatar worshippers in Madras to Maori followers of Ratana in New Zealand – to a common religion. Some ninety per cent of the worldwide Bahá'í population now live in developing countries, whereas Westerners comprise about five per cent and Middle Easterners (mostly Iranians) make up the remainder. Growth rates in Western Europe, North America and the Middle East remain below those of Africa, Asia, Eastern Europe and Australasia.

QUALIFICATIONS FOR BAHÁ'Í MEMBERSHIP

The prime motive should always be the response of man to God's Message, and the recognition of His Messenger. Those who declare themselves as Bahá'ís should become enchanted with the beauty of the teachings, and touched by the love of Bahá'u'lláh. The declarants need not know all the proofs, history, laws and principles of the Faith, but in the process of declaring themselves they must, in addition to catching the spark of faith, become basically informed about the Central Figures of the Faith, as well as the existence of laws they must follow and an administration they must obey.

(UNIVERSAL HOUSE OF JUSTICE)

Year	1954	1963	1968	1973	1978	1988	1998	2008
National assemblies	12	56	81	113	125	149	179	184

Growth in the number of Baha'i national assemblies worldwide, 1954-2008

Continent	No. of Bahá'ís	No. of LSAs*	LSAs per million**
Africa	2,143,000	3,412	4.2
Americas	1,459,000	2,920	3.4
Asia	3,439,000	2,322	0.6
Europe	153,000	890	1.2
Oceania	110,000	800	26.2
World	7,305,000	10,344	1.7

*LSA: local spiritual assembly.

**Number of LSAs per million of the general population in each geographical region.

Geographical distribution of Bahá'ís. Sources: *World Christian Database 2011* (for numbers), *Bahá'í World* (for LSA numbers).

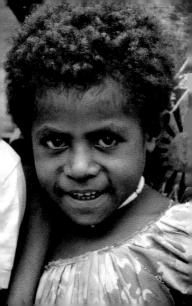

the bahá'í faith in the twenty-first century

WHEREAS THE PREVIOUS CHAPTER mainly looked at how the Bahá'í Faith is coping with external influences, this final chapter deals with aspects of its internal development. The Bahá'í community has entered the twenty-first century as a dynamic, diverse, unified, and expanding young world religion. It faces a number of challenges, but the faith's followers can generally look to its future with optimism.

left Bahá'í website on the World Wide Web http://www.bahai.org

Can the faith avoid major division?
Most major religions have split into branches, divisions, or sects. So far, however, serious schism has not occurred in the Bahá'í Faith. Small splinter groups have appeared after each leadership succession, only to fade away. Preservation of unity is especially important to Bahá'ís for two main reasons. First, unity is part of the Bahá'í mission as a divinely inspired religion. As Bahá'ís want to bring unity to the world, any serious internal division would cast doubt on the credibility of their plan. Second, Bahá'í writings condemn factionalism. Bahá'í texts state that the absence of religion is preferable to a divisive religion:

Religion must be the cause of fellowship and love. It if becomes the cause of estrangement then it is not needed, for religion is like a remedy; if it aggravates the disease then it becomes unnecessary. ('ABDU'L-BAHÁ)

In the faith's first century unity was preserved because Bahá'u'lláh and 'Abdu'l-Bahá left wills that explicitly named their successors. Bahá'ís refer to their commitment to obey these wills as 'the covenant'. The death of Shoghi Effendi in 1957 shifted authority from individuals to an internationally elected council, the Universal House of Justice, a body outlined by Bahá'u'lláh and elaborated by his successors. Nowadays, therefore, obedience to this 'covenant' refers to acceptance of its decisions and, secondarily, to the decisions of local and national councils. The messages of the House of Justice have binding authority. It is the faith's supreme law-making authority. Although it is a measure of last resort and has rarely been used, the House can revoke the membership of any Bahá'í attempting schism.

Such central authority, however, coexists with the freedom of individual Bahá'ís to express themselves and interpret scripture according to their understanding: 'Let us all remember that at the very root of the Cause lies the principle of the undoubted right of the individual to self-expression, his freedom to declare his conscience and set forth his views' (*Shoghi Effendi*). As long as no Bahá'í claims that his or her interpretation is the only correct one, debates can flourish and opinions can clash. This combination of vesting authority in elected councils and permitting individuals the freedom to express their views has allowed personal interpretation of belief within a united faith.

How might Bahá'í organization evolve?
Many procedures in Bahá'í administration were 'provisionally adopted' at the time of Shoghi Effendi's leadership and can be changed, subject to the decisions of the Universal House of Justice. These include, for example, the absence of nominations in elections, the simple plurality system (i.e. a system that elects those who receive the highest number of votes, not necessarily a majority of votes), the annual frequency of most elections, and

opposite Seat of the Universal House of Justice, Mount Carmel, Haifa.

the number of members who serve on councils. Even if changes to such features were to be legislated by the House of Justice, however, they would not become part of the faith's sacred text because such legislation can be altered by further rulings of the House of Justice itself. Indeed, Bahá'í writings distinguish between changeless sacred text and changeable legislation that is meant to ensure the continued flexibility of its organization.

What pressures are likely to determine the evolution of Bahá'í organization? They will probably include growth in membership and improvement in information technology. In many larger communities, such as in India and the USA, regional councils have already taken on many of the responsibilities previously reserved for national assemblies in order to deal with the extra work of an expanded membership. This trend towards decentralization is spreading to other communities, and it may assume additional forms in places where delegation of authority has already started. Bahá'í administration in certain countries is likely to be as influenced by developments in information technology as are the practices of other global organizations. For example, community gatherings, council meetings, training seminars and the development of educational materials have traditionally operated within confines set by transport, telephone, local libraries, the postal system and hired meeting halls. Multimedia technologies, such as the internet, are likely to lead to substantial innovation, perhaps as anticipated by Shoghi Effendi as early as the 1930s: 'A mechanism of world inter-communication will be devised, embracing the whole planet, freed from national hindrances and restrictions, and functioning with marvellous swiftness and perfect regularity.'

above House of worship, Samoa.

opposite The late King Malietoa Tanumafili II, Samoan head of state until his death in 2007, became a Bahá'í in 1968.

How might the faith's intellectual life develop?
Intellectual excellence is regarded as important both for individuals and for Bahá'í communities. The faith's writings state that individuals have been honoured with 'intellect and wisdom, the two most luminous lights in the world', and that the intellect is 'the supreme gift of God' to humanity, our 'most praiseworthy power' (*'Abdu'l-Bahá*).

Bahá'í scholars, such as Abu'l-Fadl, sustained a tradition of intellectual enquiry in Iran for more than a century. Their works, however, are known by few Bahá'ís today because they remain mostly untranslated. Western scholarly interest in the Bahá'í religion, on the other hand, flourished from the 1880s to the 1910s, notably in the works of E. G. Browne and A. L. M. Nicolas, and also V. Rosen and A. Vambery. Browne, a Cambridge orientalist, recorded his encounters with early believers in his 1893 classic *A Year Amongst the Persians*: 'Here [the student of religious thought] ... may witness ... the birth of a faith which may not impossibly win a place amidst the great religions of the world.'

ALAIN LOCKE

Alain Locke has probably been the most prominent Western intellectual Bahá'í. He was the first black Rhodes scholar, one of the founding philosophers of the 1920s Harlem Renaissance, and later professor of philosophy at Howard University. For Locke, cultural pluralism was the basis of a just democracy. He stressed the dignity of the individual and cultural differences as a protection against autocracy. As described in the passage below, Locke believed that cultural pluralism and cultural relativism were founded in the Bahá'í principle of unity in diversity:

This principle is basic in the Bahá'í teaching. It may lead us to another dangerous partisanship to assert it as exclusively Bahá'í; but there is no escaping the historical evidences of its early advocacy and its uncompromising adoption by the Bahá'í prophets and teachers ... But it is not the time for insisting on this side of the claim; the intelligent, loyal Bahá'í should stress not the source, but the importance of the idea, and rejoice not in the originality and uniqueness of the principle but rather in its prevalence and practicality. The idea has to be translated into every province of modern life and thought.

above Alain Locke

opposite Her Majesty Queen Elizabeth II is met by a delegation of British Bahá'ís at a special multifaith gathering to mark her Diamond Jubilee in 2012.

Publication of the works of H. M. Balyuzi, a Bahá'í historian, and the formation of the Association for Bahá'í Studies in 1974, sparked a revival in scholarly studies. The Association is now an international network of over twenty regional affiliates that promotes Bahá'í studies in Bahá'í communities by holding regular conferences and publishing academic journals, multi-author books, and monographs.

Despite examples of outstanding scholars and a revived interest in Bahá'í studies the religion still lacks systematic studies of its belief and thought. Until very recently there was little work relating Bahá'í social teaching to contemporary issues. Some important studies of early history have been produced in English. Scholarly interest remains confined to a minority of Bahá'ís. Further progress will require the provision of better resources for scholars (such as the establishment of additional centres with libraries, research funds and the translation of texts currently unavailable in English) as well as further cultivation by the Bahá'í community of a culture of learning and tolerance.

What will the Bahá'í Faith's relationship be with other religions?

It seems unlikely that 'triumphalism', 'fundamentalism', 'exclusivism', or the like will affect the large majority of Bahá'ís, as the faith's scriptures clearly condemn such attitudes of superiority. Indeed, as well as accepting the divine origin of world religions, Bahá'ís are encouraged to befriend the followers of other faiths. It is perhaps remarkable that, despite more than 150 years of persecution in Iran, Bahá'ís there and elsewhere continue to uphold, and sometimes to defend publicly, the validity of Islam. According to the late John Hick, an eminent Christian philosopher and theologian:

The most explicit teaching of pluralism as religious truth comes from the region between the East and the West, namely Iran (Persia). It was here that the nineteenth-century prophet Bahá'u'lláh taught that the ultimate divine reality is in itself beyond the grasp of the human mind, but has nevertheless been imaged and responded to in different historically and culturally conditioned ways by founders of the different faith-traditions; and the Bahá'í religion which he founded continues to teach this message in many countries today.

Recent developments suggest that the Bahá'í contribution to collaboration between religions will take several directions. First, Bahá'ís have been asked to act as neutral arbiters in several religious disputes. For example, in 1997 an Israeli boy killed in sectarian conflict was finally buried in a Bahá'í cemetery after Jewish and Christian leaders could not agree on the child's religious affiliation. A second way that Bahá'ís might promote cooperation between religions and between cultures is through a genuine appreciation of the riches of cultural and religious diversity, and a willingness to overcome their personal prejudices. For example, in 1994 a supreme court judge in India, in making his judgment on the dispute over the destruction of the Babri mosque in Ayodhya, cited the example of the ability of Bahá'ís from Hindu and Muslim backgrounds to live in harmony. Also, Bahá'í gatherings regularly feature performances and artistic displays by people from many different religious, racial and national backgrounds. Perhaps the varied artistic programme of the largest of all Bahá'í gatherings yet – the 1992 World Congress in New York, attended by more than 25,000 Bahá'ís – has been the best example of that trend. Finally, Bahá'ís acknowledge the spiritual contribution of native peoples. Although their exact identities have been lost to history, messengers of God who preached to indigenous peoples in the Americas and elsewhere are, in principle, recognized in Bahá'í writings.

The future

The Bahá'í view of the future of the human race is an optimistic one, a vision that arises from the faith's belief in social progress and in the ability of different people to live in harmony when inspired by ethical and spiritual teachings. In 1936 Shoghi Effendi outlined some aspects of this remarkable vision:

National rivalries, hatred and intrigues will cease, and racial animosity and prejudice will be replaced by racial amity, understanding and cooperation. The causes of religious strife will be permanently removed, economic barriers and restrictions will be completely abolished, and the inordinate distinction between classes will be obliterated. Destitution on the one hand, and gross accumulation of ownership on the other, will disappear. The enormous energy dissipated and wasted on war, whether economic or political, will be consecrated to such ends as will extend the range of human inventions and technical development, to the increase of the productivity of mankind, to the extermination of disease, to the extension of scientific research, to the raising of the standard of physical health, to the sharpening and refinement of the human brain, to the exploitation of the unused and unsuspected resources of the planet, to the prolongation of human life, and to the furtherance of any other agency that can stimulate the intellectual, moral and spiritual life of the entire human race.

Further reading

We recommend the works listed below for further information about the Bahá'í Faith. The statements of the central figures quoted in this book are from authenticated and published writings, except some of the lectures of 'Abdu'l-Bahá that were later transcribed, translated and published as books.

General books

Momen, M. *The Bahá'í Faith: A Beginner's Guide.* Oxford: Oneworld Publications, 2007

Momen, M. *Bahá'u'lláh: A Short Biography.* Oxford: Oneworld Publications, 2007

Smith, P. *The Bahá'í Faith: A Short History.* Oxford: Oneworld Publications, 1996

Smith, P. *A Concise Encyclopedia of the Bahá'í Faith.* Oxford: Oneworld Publications, 1999

Bahá'í writings

'Abdu'l-Bahá. *Selections from the Writings of 'Abdu'l-Bahá.* Compiled by the Research Department of the Universal House of Justice. Trans. Bahá'í World Centre. Haifa: Bahá'í World Centre, 1978

Bahá'u'lláh. *Gleanings from the Writings of Bahá'u'lláh.* Trans. Shoghi Effendi. 2nd edn, Wilmette: Bahá'í Publishing Trust, 1976

——. *The Hidden Words.* Trans. Shoghi Effendi. Oxford: Oneworld Publications, 1986

——. *The Seven Valleys.* Trans. A. K. Khan and M. Gail. London: Nightingale Books, 1992

——. *The Book of Certitude.* Trans. Shoghi Effendi. 2nd edn, Wilmette: Bahá'í Publishing Trust, 1950

Bahá'u'lláh, the Báb and 'Abdu'l-Bahá. *Bahá'í Prayers.* Wilmette: Bahá'í Publishing Trust, 1991

Books on Bahá'í history

Balyuzi, H. *'Abdu'l-Bahá: The Centre of the Covenant of Bahá'u'lláh.* Rev. edn, Oxford: George Ronald, 1987

Balyuzi, H. *Bahá'u'lláh: The King of Glory.* 2nd rev. edn, Oxford: George Ronald, 1991

Shoghi Effendi. *God Passes By.* Rev. edn, Wilmette: Bahá'í Publishing Trust, 1974

Smith, P. *An introduction to the Baha'i Faith.* Cambridge: Cambridge University Press, 2008

Specialist reading

Badiee, J. *An Earthly Paradise: Bahá'í Houses of Worship Around the World.* Oxford: George Ronald, 1992

Brookshaw, D. and Fazel, S., eds. *The Baha'is of Iran: Socio-historical Studies.* Abingdon & New York: Routledge, 2008

Collins, W. 'Bahá'í Family Life: Beyond the Traditional'. In *Search for Values: Ethics in Bahá'í Thought,* eds. S. Fazel and J. Danesh. Los Angeles: Kalimat Press, 2004

Fazel, S. 'Inter-religious Dialogue and the Bahá'í Faith: Some Preliminary Observations'. In *Revisioning the Sacred: New Perspectives on a Bahá'í Theology,* Studies in the Babi and Bahá'í Religions, vol. 8, ed. J. A. McLean. Los Angeles: Kalimat Press, 1997

Momen, M. 'Relativism: A Basis for Bahá'í Metaphysics'. In *Studies in Honor of the Late Hasan M. Balyuzi,* Studies in the Babi and Bahá'í Religions, vol. 5, ed. M. Momen. Los Angeles: Kalimat Press, 1988

Ruhe, D. *Door of Hope: A Century of the Bahá'í Faith in the Holy Land.* Rev. edn, Oxford: George Ronald, 1986

Thomas, R. *Racial Unity: An Imperative for Social Progress.* Rev. edn, Ottawa: Association for Bahá'í Studies, 1993

The Universal House of Justice. *The Promise of World Peace.* Oxford: Oneworld, 1986

White, C. 'Prayer as Remembrance'. In *Reason and Revelation: New Directions in Baha'i Thought,* Studies in the Babi and Baha'i Religions, vol. 13, eds. S. Fazel and J. Danesh. Los Angeles: Kalimat Press, 2002

Useful websites

Information on the Bahá'í Faith, its history and literature, can also be found on the internet. An excellent starting point is the home page of the Bahá'í World Centre: www.bahai.org and that of the BBC: www.bbc.co.uk/religion/religions/bahai. Bahá'í scriptures and other relevant texts are also available at www.reference.bahai.org and www.bahai-library.org.

Index

Abbott, Robert 141

Abdul-Aziz, Sultan 66, **69**

'Abdu'l-Bahá [Abbás Effendi] 31, 40, 44–5,
    45, **46**, **47**, 58, 87, 109, 134, 139, 141
    and other religions 79
    Paris Talks 44
    prayers 92
    The Secret of Divine Civilization 70
    Some Answered Questions 44
    Tablet to The Hague 132
    Will and Testament 45, 48
    writings of 70

Abu'l-Fadl 151

Akka 40, **40**, **43**, **46**, **52**, 108

Alexander II, Tsar 66, **68**

the arts 115–26
    art and artists 120–3
    houses of worship **85**, 115, **115**, 116, **116–19**,
        151
    music 120, 126
    poetry 124
    pottery **115**, 123

Association for Bahá'í Studies 152

the Báb [Sayyid Ali Muhammad] 31, 32–3, **34**, 38
    The Exposition 32, 70
    letters to world leaders 70
    writings of 70

Bahá'í administrative order 51, 105–7, 148–50
    Auxiliary Board Members 51, 105, 107
    Counsellors 105, 107
    evolution of 148–51
    Hands of the Cause of God 51
    spiritual assemblies 49, 51, 103, 105, 106,
        139, 144, 151
    Universal House of Justice 48, 51, 105, 109,
        132, 134, 139, 148, 151

Bahá'í community life 97, 102–4
    consultation 97, 103, 106
    devotional meetings 92, 97, 102, 104
    holy days 102, 104, 106
    nineteen-day feasts 97, 102, 106

study circles 97, 104, 109

Bahá'í Faith
    and Christianity 9, 44, 76
    expansion of 143–4
    future development of 148–54
    geographical distribution of 9–10, **12–13**, 51,
        143–4
    institutions of 97
    and Islam 9, 76, 131, 153
    pioneering 143
    and Judaism 9
    and other religions 153–4
    study of 152
    and United Nations 134
    unity within 10–11, 148
    website 147
    see also practices of the Bahá'í Faith; teachings
    of the Bahá'í Faith

Bahá'í World Centre 49, 108–9, **108**, **109**, 110,
    111
    collection of sacred texts 57
    International Bahá'í Archives building **35**, 109,
        109
    International Teaching Centre 107
    and pilgrimage 108, 111
    Shrine of the Báb **8**, **30**, **34**, **35**, 49, **85**, 109,
        109
    Shrine of Bahá'u'lláh 40

Bahá'í World Congresses **106**, **107**, 154

Bahá'u'lláh [Mirza Husayn Ali Nuri] 9, 18, 31,
    38–41, 51, 57, 73, 76, 108–9, 134
    Book of Certitude 39, 42, 49, 58, 62, 64–5, 76
    Book of the Covenant 44, 58
    Hidden Words **42**, 49, **57**, 58, 59–60
    letters to world leaders 39, 58, 66–9
    Most Holy Book 40, 58, 87
    and other religions 79
    prayers 92, 94
    Seven Valleys 38, 61
    Tablet of Carmel 108
    Tablet to the Kings 66

as universal messiah 76
    writings 57, 61

Bahiyyih Khanum 139

Balyuzi, H. M. 152

Bell, Alexander Graham 44, **45**

Ben Gurion, David 49

Ben Zvi, Itzhak 51

Blomfield, Lady Sara Louise 78, **138**

Browne, E. G. 40, 41, **41**, 44, 132, 151

Buddha, the 18, 31, 73, 76

Carnegie, Andrew 44, **45**

Conference of Living Religions within the British
    Empire 78

Djalili, Omid 126, **126**

donations to Bahá'í funds 112

Du Bois, W. E. B. 44

Esperantists 134, 138

Esslemont, John **52**

fasting 85, 92, 112

Forel, August **24**

Franz Joseph, Emperor 66, **68**

Galtung, Johan 134

Gibran, Kahlil 44

Gillespie, Dizzy **125**, 126

God 9, 16, 18, 59, 62, 65, 73–4, 88
    and human history 9, 18, 74
    nature of 73, 74
    and prophets/messengers 18, 31, 62, 70, 73,
        74, 76–7, 154

'Golden Rule' 78, 80–1

Gregory, Louis 141, **141**

Gregory, Louisa 141, **141**

Haifa **46**, **47**, 108
    see also Bahá'í World Centre

Hayden, Robert 124, **124**, 141

Hick, John 153

interfaith dialogue 78–9

International Bahá'í Council 51

Iran
    and the Báb 31–3, 49
    and Bahá'í education 130–1, 135, 139

and Bahá'ís 139, 143, 153

and Bahá'u'lláh 31, 38–9

destruction of National Bahá'í Centre **130**

persecution of Bahá'ís 33, 129, 130–2, **130**, 134, 140, 153

Jesus Christ 18, 31, 62, 73, 76

Jordan, David 134

Khadijih Khanum 34

King, Coretta Scott 142

Leach, Bernard **115**, 123, **123**

Locke, Alain 141, 152, **152**

Locke, Kevin **122**, 126

Malietoa Tanumafili II, King **150**

Marie of Romania, Queen **50**, 139

meditation 85, 92, 93

and reading scripture 92

Mirza Buzurg **42**

Mishkin-Qalam 57, 126

Moses 18, 76

Muhammad 18, 76

Munirih Khanum **46**

Napoleon III, Emperor 66, 67, **69**

Nasir-Din Shah 66, **68**, 132

National Association for the Advancement of Colored People 134

Nicolas, A. L. M. 151

Pankhurst, Emmeline 44, **45**

persecution of Bahá'ís

and destruction of sacred texts 70

in Iran 33, 129, 130–2, **130**, **132**, 134, 140, 153

by Muslims 131

in the Ottoman Empire 67, 132

Western protests against 67, 132

Pius IX, Pope 66, **69**

prayer 74, 85, 87, 92, 94, 112

prophets (messengers) of God 18, 31, 62, 70, 73, 74, 76–7

Rabbani, Madame Ruhiyyih 51, **51**, 133

Race Amity Conference **142**

Roosevelt, Theodore 44, **45**

Root, Martha **139**

sacred texts of the Bahá'í Faith 44, 49, 57–70, 139, 151

Book of Certitude (Bahá'u'lláh) 39, 42, 49, 58, 62, 64–5, 76

Book of the Covenant (Bahá'u'lláh) 44, 58

Hidden Words (Bahá'u'lláh) **42**, 49, **57**, 58, 59–60

letters to world leaders (the Báb) 70

letters to world leaders (Bahá'u'lláh) 39, 58, 66–9

Most Holy Book (Bahá'u'lláh) 40, 58, 87

Paris Talks ('Abdu'l-Bahá) 44

The Secret of Divine Civilization ('Abdu'l-Bahá) 70

Seven Valleys (Bahá'u'lláh) 38, 61

Some Answered Questions ('Abdu'l-Bahá) 44

Tablet of Carmel (Bahá'u'lláh) 108

Tablet to The Hague ('Abdu'l-Bahá) 132

Tablet to the Kings (Bahá'u'lláh) 66

Will and Testament ('Abdu'l-Bahá) 45, 48

St Barbe Baker, Richard **24**

Seals and Croft 126, **126**

Shoghi Effendi 31, 45, 48–51, **48**, **52**, **53**, 109, 141, 154

God Passes By 49

World Order of Bahá'u'lláh 49

Tahirih 139, 140

teachings of the Bahá'í Faith 9, 10, 15–28

on the afterlife 15, 16, 88–91

on the Bible 62

on charity 28, 112, 135

on detachment 28

on education 27, 135, 138–9

and equality of the sexes 15, 22, 129, 131, 135, 138–9

on freedom 15, 26–8

on good deeds 21, 32, 36, 59, 60, 61, 78, 89, 135

on harmony 15, 20–5

on health, healing and diet 87

on human nature 9, 10, 15, 16

on human rights 15, 27, 44

on marriage and family life 96, 98–9, 138

on other religions 74, 78–9, 153

on peace 10, 132–4

on progress 15, 16–19

on prophets/messengers of God 18, 31, 62, 73, 74, 76–7, 154

on purpose of life 15, 74, 88, 89, 134

on purpose of religion 18, 26, 74, 82

on race 20–1, 129, 141–2

on reason 24, 26, 85, 88, 99, 151

on relativity of religious truth 18, 20, 57, 74

on religious freedom 28

on revelation 18, 58, 82

on science and religion 15, 19, 24–5

on selflessness/detachment 16, 24, 25, 27, 28, 64, 89, 92

on social issues 15, 19, 61, 66, 70, 78, 86, 106, 108, 129, 134–7

on social history 19

on the soul 15, 16, 85, 88, 90

on spiritual development 15, 16, 18, 19, 25, 26, 28, 61, 74, 82, 85, 88, 92, 94

on tobacco, alcohol and drugs 85, 86

on truth 18, 57, 74, 88, 131, 143

on virtues 16, 22, 28, 59, 98, 112, world order 20, 49, 54

Thoresen, Lasse 126

Tobey, Mark 120–1, **120**, **121**, 123

Turvey, Reginald 123, **123**

Universal House of Justice 48, 51, 148, **149**, 151

The Promise of World Peace 132–4, 141

The Prosperity of Humankind 134

Turning Point for All Nations 134

Universal Races Congress 141

Victoria, Queen 66, 67, **69**

Villasenor, David **122**

Wilhelm I, Kaiser 66, 67, **68**

Zamenhof, Lidia **138**, 139

Zoroaster 31